REPTILES
AND DINOSAURS

Britannica Illustrated Science Library

Encyclopædia Britannica, Inc.

Chicago ▪ London ▪ New Delhi ▪ Paris ▪ Seoul ▪ Sydney ▪ Taipei ▪ Tokyo

Britannica Illustrated Science Library

Idea and Concept of This Work: Editorial Sol 90

Project Management: Fabián Cassan

Photo Credits: Corbis, ESA, Getty Images, Graphic News, NASA, National Geographic, Science Photo Library

Illustrators: Guido Arroyo, Pablo Aschei, Gustavo J. Caironi, Hernán Cañellas, Leonardo César, José Luis Corsetti, Vanina Farías, Joana Garrido, Celina Hilbert, Isidro López, Diego Martín, Jorge Martínez, Marco Menco, Ala de Mosca, Diego Mourelos, Pablo Palastro, Eduardo Pérez, Javier Pérez, Ariel Piroyansky, Ariel Roldán, Marcel Socías, Néstor Taylor, Trebol Animation, Juan Venegas, Coralia Vignau, 3DN, 3DOM studio, Jorge Ivanovich, Fernando Ramallo, Constanza Vicco

Composition and Pre-press Services: Editorial Sol 90

Translation Services and Index: Publication Services, Inc.

Britannica Illustrated Science Library Staff

Editorial
Michael Levy, *Executive Editor, Core Editorial*
John Rafferty, *Associate Editor, Earth Sciences*
William L. Hosch, *Associate Editor, Mathematics and Computers*
Kara Rogers, *Associate Editor, Life Sciences*
Rob Curley, *Senior Editor, Science and Technology*
David Hayes, *Special Projects Editor*

Art and Composition
Steven N. Kapusta, *Director*
Carol A. Gaines, *Composition Supervisor*
Christine McCabe, *Senior Illustrator*

Media Acquisition
Kathy Nakamura, *Manager*

Copy Department
Sylvia Wallace, *Director*
Julian Ronning, *Supervisor*

Information Management and Retrieval
Sheila Vasich, *Information Architect*

Production Control
Marilyn L. Barton

Manufacturing
Kim Gerber, *Director*

Encyclopædia Britannica, Inc.

Jacob E. Safra, *Chairman of the Board*

Jorge Aguilar-Cauz, *President*

Michael Ross, *Senior Vice President, Corporate Development*

Dale H. Hoiberg, *Senior Vice President and Editor*

Marsha Mackenzie, *Director of Production*

International Standard Book Number (set):
978-1-59339-382-3
International Standard Book Number (volume):
978-1-59339-395-3
Britannica Illustrated Science Library:
Reptiles and Dinosaurs 2008

Printed in China

ENCYCLOPÆDIA
Britannica®

www.britannica.com

Reptiles and Dinosaurs

Contents

NAGA RASSA MASK
This mask is used during popular festivals in Sri Lanka to frighten evil spirits. In Asian cultures, nagas represent sacred serpents.

Feared and Worshipped

B ecause of their frightening appearances, snakes, dragons, and crocodiles are found in the legends and myths of peoples throughout the world. In sculptures, paintings, and masks used for various ceremonies, many of these animals are represented as good or bad gods or are associated with magical powers. The snake is usually linked to the primordial waters from which life was created. In Asia, it is said that nagas (sacred serpents) are descended from Kasyapa, the father of all life. Consequently, it is common during popular festivals for both men and women to dance disguised with masks that represent these animals in order to frighten away evil spirits and seek protection. Certain Papuan peoples believe that crocodiles have special powers, and in Europe, mythical winged dragons that breathe fire are viewed as the guardians of treasures. Throughout history, these animals have been both feared and respected, objects of fascination and passion. The purpose of this book is to reveal, in detail, what reptiles are really like. Here you will find clear, precise information about the appearance and behavior of reptiles, including dinosaurs—a group of reptiles that dominated the globe for millions of years. This fascinating book, which features specially prepared illustrations and images, will reveal details about these creatures as if they were alive on these pages.

Did you know that reptiles were the first vertebrates to become totally independent of aquatic environments? This was made possible by the emergence of the amniotic egg. Its shell and membranes enabled reptilian young to develop on land without the need to return to water. Today there are about 8,200 classified species of reptiles in a wide variety of shapes and sizes. These species include turtles, lizards, snakes, crocodiles, and tuataras. Clues about the lives of many of these animals can be found by examining their feet. Different species use their feet to scale walls, climb slender stalks, or run across loose, hot sand dunes. Some reptiles live underground, while others prefer the surface. Since their body temperature is variable, reptiles tend to spend many hours in the sun exposed to direct solar rays and infrared radiation released from heated surfaces.

With their long, narrow bodies, snakes are different from all other reptiles because they have long spines with many vertebrae. Although they cannot hear in the way mammals do, they can detect low-frequency vibrations in the soil that reveal the presence of predators or prey. Most snakes are carnivorous and can eat objects larger than their own bodies. Stealthy, undulating crawling, sudden color changes, and oversized jaws are other identifying characteristics of reptiles— amazing animals with extraordinary traits that have enabled them to survive for millions of years.

Each page of this book will help you to become familiar with these creatures that are so different from humans. Some of them give birth to completely developed young. They are not born fragile and immature, dependent on their parents to feed and take care of them, as most mammals are. Reptile species also vary widely in the types of scales they have. Their scales may have defensive knobs and spines, as is the case with the tails of some lizards, or they may form crests along their necks, backs, or tails.

Although snakes are some of the most commonly feared animals, only one out of ten is dangerous. Few people know that snakes are timid creatures that prefer to stay hidden. Most snakes will never attack unless they feel threatened and use warning mechanisms and behaviors before attacking. Unfortunately, others are poisonous—so most snakes are hated and persecuted. The process of learning more about them and learning to identify the really dangerous ones may help us to keep them from disappearing. Many reptile species today are in danger of extinction because of indiscriminate hunting and habitat destruction. Not only ecologists but all people must be concerned about their welfare, helping to ensure that they continue to be part of life on Earth. ●

Dinosaurs

During the 170 million years from the late Triassic Period to the late Cretaceous Period, an extraordinary group of animals, called the dinosaurs, dominated the Earth. Some were small, but others were gigantic. Some ate only plants and had long necks, and others had sharp teeth. Currently we are increasingly well-informed about dinosaurs because of the

findings of paleontologists, who study the fossilized teeth and bones of these animals. Sometime during the late Cretaceous Period, dinosaurs disappeared from the face of the planet in an event known as the K-T extinction event. Some attribute the dinosaurs' disappearance to the impact of a large meteorite with the Earth. In this chapter, you will find very detailed illustrations of these prehistoric creatures.●

Terrible Lizards

D inosaurs dominated the Earth for 170 million years, from the late Triassic to the late Cretaceous periods, when the supercontinents of Laurasia and Gondwana were splitting into the landmasses of today. The mass extinction of the dinosaurs about 65 million years ago left fossil remains, including footprints, eggs, and bones. Finding these fossils has enabled scientists to study and classify dinosaurs and to learn about their posture, size, diet, and many other aspects of their lives. These studies revealed that this prehistoric group of lizards included herbivores and carnivores of extraordinary size and striking shapes. ●

Flexible Neck
Moved more
easily because the
vertebrae were
light in weight

Legs

 Depending on their lifestyle, some dinosaurs walked on two legs, and some walked on four. However, they all had a similar posture. Due to the structure of their legs, they bear little resemblance to their relatives today: lizards, tuataras, turtles, snakes, and crocodiles.

DEINOS SAURO
Terrible   Lizard

IDENTITY
The term Dinosauria was proposed for these extinct reptiles by paleontologist Richard Owen in 1842. The name of each species is based on characteristics of its shape and physiology, the name of its discoverer, or the location where it was found.

BAROSAURUS
or "heavy reptile"

① LIZARDS
The limbs project outward. At the elbows and knees, the legs are bent at right angles. This arrangement is called extended posture.

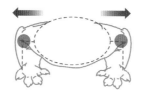

② CROCODILES
These animals have semi-extended posture. The limbs project out and down. The elbows and knees are bent at a 45° angle. These species crawl slowly and straighten up to run.

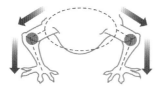

③ DINOSAURS
These animals had erect posture. The limbs project below the body. Both the elbows and the knees are beneath the body.

GOLDEN YEARS

From the primitive dinosaurs of the Triassic Period, evolutionary lines of carnivores and herbivores diverged. Later in the Jurassic and Cretaceous periods large herbivores and fierce carnivores dominated the landscape, living under environmental conditions that favored enormous diversity in body forms and feeding behaviors—until their extinction.

Herrerasaurus
Length: 13 feet (4 m)

Coelophysis
Length: 9.2 feet (2.8 m)

Eoraptor
Length: 3 feet (1 m)

Mussaurus
Length: 6.6 feet (2 m)

Plateosaurus
Length: 26 feet (8 m)

Dryosaurus
Length: 13 feet (4 m)

Megalosaurus
Length: 29.5 feet (9 m)

Brachiosaurus
Length: 82 feet (25 m)

TRIASSIC PERIOD 251-199.6 MILLION YEARS AGO

JURASSIC PERIOD 199.6-145.5 MILLION YEARS AGO

Marsh vs. Cope

The American paleontologists Othniel C. Marsh and Edward D. Cope faced off in a very peculiar struggle. They competed to determine who could find more dinosaur bones and species. The competition was plagued with corruption, mutual accusations of espionage, fraud, theft, and even personal violence. Marsh considered himself the winner of "Bone Wars," but the field of paleontology was the real winner as roughly 130 species were identified between the two rivals.

SIR DINOSAUR
Sir Richard Owen, a British paleontologist, was the first to identify fossil remains of "terrible lizards," or "monstrous lizards." He proposed the term Dinosauria, based on his studies and discoveries, and made the first reconstruction of a fossil for the great London Exhibition of 1851.

Saurischians

These dinosaurs had hip bones similar to those of today's reptiles, such as crocodiles and lizards. Many species of saurischian dinosaurs have been found, including *Velociraptor* and *Argentinosaurus*. They had long, flexible necks and large claws on the initial digits.

Lizard Hip
Pelvic structure of saurischian dinosaurs

FIERCE LIZARDS
Carnivores of the Cretaceous Period. They grew up to 46 feet (14 m) long and weighed up to 7.7 tons (7 metric tons). Their teeth were like knives.

Tyrannosaurus rex

SUBORDER	INFRAORDER
Theropoda	**Ceratosauria** *Coelophysis bauri*
	Tetanurae *Allosaurus fragilis*
Sauropodomorpha	**Prosauropoda** *Plateosaurus engelhardti*
	Sauropoda *Argentinosaurus huinculensis*

Ornithischians

Herbivores with hip bones structured like those of birds. The pubis slants backward, parallel to the ischium. Some of the most famous ornithischians were *Triceratops* and *Parasaurolophus*. Some ornithischians were protected from head to tail by bony plates.

They Only Look Alike
In spite of their name, these animals are not ancestors of today's birds.

ORNITHISCHIANS
Named for the curvature in their thighbones. They could walk on two legs.

Camptosaurus sp.

SUBORDER	INFRAORDER
Thyreophora	**Scelidosauria** *Trimucrodon cuneatus*
	Stegosauria *Stegosaurus armatus*
	Ankylosauria *Centrosaurus* sp.
Cerapoda	**Marginocephalia** *Triceratops prorsus*
	Euornithopoda *Pisanosaurus mertii*

110 tons
(100 metric tons)

ESTIMATED WEIGHT OF AN *ARGENTINOSAURUS*

Over 2,000

SPECIES OF DINOSAURS HAVE BEEN CATALOGED AT PRESENT.

| *Stegosaurus* Length: 30 feet (9 m) | *Camarasaurus* Length: 66 feet (20 m) | *Therizinosaurus* Length: 39 feet (12 m) | *Caudipteryx* Length: 3 feet (1 m) | *Suchomimus* Length: 43 feet (13 m) | *Giganotosaurus* Length: 49 feet (15 m) | *Corythosaurus* Length: 33 feet (10 m) |

CRETACEOUS PERIOD 145.5–65.5 MILLION YEARS AGO

The Triassic Period

The biological crisis of the late Permian Period was followed by a slow resurgence of life in the Triassic Period. The Mesozoic Era has commonly been called the "Age of Reptiles," and its most famous members are the dinosaurs. In the earliest part of the period, the first representatives of today's amphibians appeared, and toward the end of the period the first mammals emerged. In the middle to late Triassic Period, the many families of ferns and conifers appeared that continue to exist today, as well as other groups of plants that are now extinct. ●

THE TRIAS
were named in 1834 by German paleontologist Friedrich August von Alberti, who in doing so grouped the three rock formations that defined this period.

VEGETATION
Giant conifers were among the trees that lived on Pangea.

Flora

Pangea was mostly a dry, hot desert with palm trees, ginkgoes, and other gymnosperms. Some small species of horsetail rushes (genus *Equisetum*), ferns, and marine algae also survived there.

EXTINCTION
Toward the end of this period, a new extinction event removed several groups of species while opening up new horizons for those that survived—especially the dinosaurs, which spread rapidly.

A New World

After the extinction of nearly 95 percent of all life at the end of the Permian Period, the Earth was a dry place with hot deserts and rocky areas. Only the coasts had enough moisture for plants to grow. There was only one continent, called Pangea, which was surrounded by a single ocean, Panthalassa. This supercontinent was the home of dinosaurs and other animals.

250 TO 203

MILLION YEARS AGO

The Earth had only one continental mass, called Pangea. This continent had an upper region called Laurasia and a lower region called Gondwana. The two areas were partly separated by the Tethys Sea, which later almost completely disappeared.

GREENHOUSE EFFECT
A rapid, extreme global warming event is one of several possible causes of the great extinction of the late Permian Period. It could have created the hot, dry climate that prevailed during the Triassic Period.

NUMEROUS SPECIES
Reptiles and mammals flourished alongside the dinosaurs.

FIRST COUSINS
In addition to the dinosaurs, the pterosaurs—winged dinosaurs—and *Lagosuchus* lived during the Triassic Period. Together these three types of animals make up the Ornithodira group, though this is often debated today.

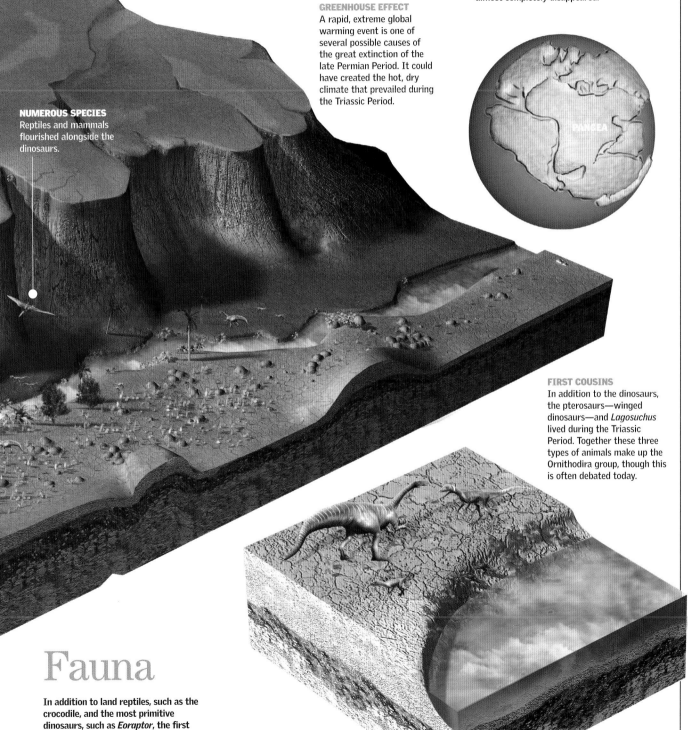

PANGEA

Fauna

In addition to land reptiles, such as the crocodile, and the most primitive dinosaurs, such as *Eoraptor*, the first mammals appeared during this period.

The "Age of Reptiles"

The first period of the Mesozoic Era gave rise to the "Age of Reptiles." On land, the synapsids, which later developed into mammals, began to decline, and the archosaurs, or "dominant reptiles," lived in various habitats. The earliest crocodiles began to develop, along with turtles and frogs, among others. The pterosaurs ruled the air and the ichthyosaurs the water. The dinosaurs—another order of archosaurs—appeared in the Middle Triassic, approximately 250 million years ago. Toward the end of the Triassic Period, many other reptiles declined dramatically, and the dinosaurs began their reign.●

The First Dinosaurs

The most primitive dinosaurs were very small in comparison to their relatives of later epochs. Most of them have been found in South America. They were carnivores. Some were scavengers, and others were highly agile hunters. They shared very primitive morphological structures with other reptiles of their group, the archosaurs. Mixed with these primitive structures, however, were advanced bone forms similar to those of the predators that would dominate the Cretaceous Period. These predators were known as the theropods. Throughout the Triassic Period, the early dinosaurs were an uncommon subgroup of reptiles. Toward the end of the Triassic Period, the first large herbivores appeared.

Eoraptor

Eoraptor fossils were discovered in 1991 in northwestern Argentina. This small carnivore lived 228 million years ago and measured up to 40 inches (1 m) long. It had sharp teeth and agile hind legs for running and chasing its prey. It may also have eaten carrion.

EORAPTOR
Tiny predator whose name means "thief of dawn"

HOLLOW SHAPE
is what *Coelophysis* means.

TAIL
Most predators used their tails to keep their balance while chasing their prey.

SPINAL COLUMN
The central vertebrae are high and short, and the neural arches have square-shaped projections that are thicker toward the back. There are only two sacral vertebrae.

Mussaurus

The only known fossils of this species were found alongside eggshells. They were no more than 8 inches (20 cm) long. Their adult size is unknown, but it is estimated to have been as much as 6.5 to 8 feet (2-2.5 m). They are known to have been herbivores.

Coelophysis

This skilled carnivore could grow up to 9.2 feet (2.8 m) long. Two types of fossils have been found. They are believed to be males and females, respectively. Fossils of this biped hunter have been found in the United States in several southwestern states.

MUSSAURUS
means "rat reptile."

HERRERASAURUS

Herrerasaurus ischigualastensis

Size	13 feet (4 m)
Diet	Carnivorous
Habitat	Conifer Forests
Epoch	Late Triassic
Range	South America

DIFFERENT SIZES

Mussaurus **Eoraptor** **Coelophysis** **Herrerasaurus**

Herrerasaurus

is one of the most ancient dinosaurs. It is considered a key to understanding the path dinosaurs took to dominate the following 160 million years. The first fossils were found in the early 1960s in the Ischigualasto valley in northern Argentina by an official paleontological commission headed by Osvaldo Reig. He named the dinosaur in honor of the local guide who found it. Since then several complete skeletons have been found.

A TRUE CARNIVORE
One of the traits that defined this animal as a dinosaur was its typical theropodian head. Its narrow skull had nasal cavities in the front part of its snout, and its eye sockets were part of a hollow bony structure, making its skull both lightweight and strong.

MOUTH
Its tubelike teeth were more curved than those of other carnivores that followed, but they were sharp and serrated like those of its theropod relatives.

LIMBS FOR HUNTING
Like its head, this dinosaur's limbs had the same proportions as the later giant predators of the Cretaceous Period. Its small front limbs were designed for capturing prey.

FRONT LIMBS
The relative size of its front limbs suggests that this animal mainly walked on two feet. Each hand had three long claws and two short ones. Its hands were able to grasp with the help of "thumbs" slightly opposed to the other claws. Its hand was a formidable weapon for attacking and holding prey, an earlier form of the hands of other theropods.

Thumbs

PELVIS
Herrerasaurus was a very early saurischian with a primitive sacrum, ilium, and hind legs but a highly developed pubic bone and vertebrae. These traits show that this dinosaur had unique characteristics in its spinal column.

HIND LEGS
On its lower limbs, this dinosaur's toe bones show a high degree of superposition. The toe bones of the first digit, although well developed, are very short and lightweight compared to the second, third, and fourth toes. These long, strong feet enabled *Herrerasaurus* to run while bearing the great weight of its body.

V
IV
III
II
I

220 pounds (100 kg)

An adult *Herrerasaurus* weighed between 220 and 880 pounds (100-400 kg).

The First Giant Herbivore

This primitive saurischian was among the first to usher in the age of the dinosaurs in the late Triassic Period, about 210 million years ago. Dinosaurs had already been in existence for some time, but they were smaller predators thus far. The saurischian was clearly one of the first that fed exclusively on plants and that reached the immense sizes typical of herbivores. Many fossils have been found in over 50 separate locations. The secret of this dinosaur's survival is believed to have been the lack of competition for food, since no other herbivore of the time grew as large. Its name, which means "lizard-hipped," was given to it in 1837 by the German naturalist Hermann von Meyer. ●

Plateosaurus engelhardti

These prosauropods, of the suborder Sauropodomorpha, were among the primitive herbivorous dinosaurs that were forerunners of the giant sauropods of the Jurassic Period. However, they were not actually ancestors of these animals. It is known that they associated with others of their own species because, in many areas, several specimens have been found together. Because of the hot, dry conditions that prevailed where they lived, it seems that they migrated constantly in search of food, which consisted of conifers and palm trees.

SEXUAL DIMORPHISM
It is thought that *Plateosaurus* varied in size according to its environment. There is also evidence that males and females had different shapes.

Movement
It moved about on its four muscular legs, but it could probably stand up on its hind legs and run quickly.

EVENTUAL BIPEDS
Its powerful hips supported the entire weight of its body when it stood up on its hind legs to reach food in the high branches of trees.

Head
Its brain was small in proportion to the weight of its body, so it is not believed to have been very intelligent.

In the Treetops
Its long neck helped it to reach the tops of trees. Its mouth had pouches for storing food while it chewed.

PLATEOSAURUS
Plateosaurus engelhardti

Size	26-33 feet (8-10 m)
Diet	Herbivorous
Habitat	Semiarid Regions
Epoch	Late Triassic
Range	Europe

WHERE IT LIVED
Its fossils were found in semiarid areas of what are now Germany, France, and Switzerland. At the time, those areas were part of the supercontinent Pangea.

MATING
Plateosaurs were polyandrous, meaning that the dominant matriarch had from three to five male mates, who competed for her attention during mating season. The eggs, of various sizes, were cared for by each respective male.

WEIGHT-BEARING TOES

Upper Limb

Claw

Defensive Claw
This animal had few defensive resources. However, one of the toes of its front feet had a powerful claw that it used to cut branches and for self-defense. In reality, however, its best defense was to run.

Hind Foot

The Jurassic Period

D uring this period, dinosaurs diversified greatly and spread out to occupy land, sea, and air. Along with large herbivores, there were salamanders, lizards, and the *Archaeopteryx*, the most ancient bird known. The climate of the Jurassic Period was mild, with moisture-laden winds from the ocean. They brought great downpours, enabling forests to cover wide areas of land. ●

STUDIES IN JURA
The name "Jurassic" comes from the Jura mountain range in the northern Swiss Alps. This is where the formal mapping of the rocks of this period took place.

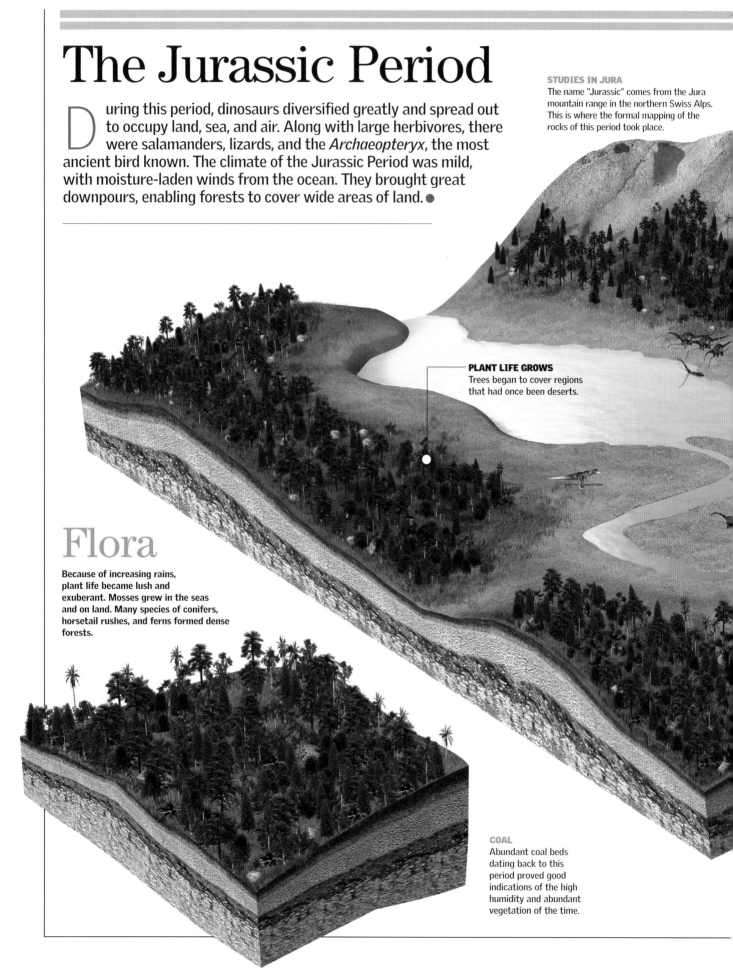

PLANT LIFE GROWS
Trees began to cover regions that had once been deserts.

Flora

Because of increasing rains, plant life became lush and exuberant. Mosses grew in the seas and on land. Many species of conifers, horsetail rushes, and ferns formed dense forests.

COAL
Abundant coal beds dating back to this period proved good indications of the high humidity and abundant vegetation of the time.

The Green Planet

As Pangea split apart, the sea level rose, and large areas of land were flooded. This process increased humidity levels, which led to intense rainfall and created a milder climate. These climate conditions helped create rich forest ecosystems. Afforded abundant food, animal populations skyrocketed. The splitting of the continent also caused volcanic eruptions. Despite the dramatic movements of tectonic plates, the climate was warm and temperate on most areas of the planet.

208 TO 140
MILLION YEARS AGO

The Earth began to divide. During the Jurassic Period, North America drifted north and separated from what is now South America. North America formed part of Laurasia with what would become Europe. Antarctica, South America, India, and Australia formed Gondwana to the south.

A NEW OCEAN
The Tethys Sea expanded from east to west, separating Laurasia and Gondwana. The Gulf of Mexico and the Atlantic Ocean began to form.

ORNITHISCHIANS
These dinosaurs were numerous on the continents.

SHARED WORLD
During this period, the first marsupials appeared. Today highly developed versions of these mammals exist in Australia, which split apart from the rest of Gondwana in the late Jurassic. The Jurassic was also the age of *Archaeopteryx*, the most ancient of the primitive birds.

Fauna

Dinosaurs greatly diversified and increased their geographic distribution during this period. Herbivorous saurischians, such as *Brachiosaurus*, and carnivores, such as *Allosaurus*, predominated. Ornithischians, such as *Stegosaurus*, also multiplied during this time.

Different Species

During the middle of the Jurassic Period, the planet was lush and green. The gradual splitting of Pangea created new ecological environments, which were more humid and more diverse. The increased humidity enabled the growth of large trees and dense vegetation. This flourishing environment powered the continued diversification of different dinosaur species. In contrast, these conditions forced a decline in the majority of synapsids, and the archosaurs —the group that includes crocodiles— largely disappeared. Other species also found their ecological niches and multiplied. These species included sea creatures, such as sharks and rays, that resemble their modern relatives, as well as ray-finned fish with sharp teeth, such as the fierce predator *Aspidorhynchus*. ●

Giants of the Mesozoic

Giant herbivores dominated the Earth. However, increasing diversity also brought increasing competition. The large sauropods, such as *Diplodocus*, and ornithischians, such as the stegosaurids, had to watch out for larger theropods, such as *Megalosaurus*, as well as for hordes of small, swift predators, such as *Compsognathus*. The first bird to descend from small dinosaurs appeared.

MEGALOSAURUS
means "large lizard."

DRYOSAURUS
means "oak reptile."

Megalosaurus

In 1676, the bones of one of the first dinosaurs were found in southern England, although they were not identified as such until 1819. This theropod predator was highly intelligent in comparison to its peers. It lived 181 million years ago, grew up to 29.5 feet (9 m) long, and weighed 1.1 tons (1 metric ton). It walked on its two hind legs and had two powerful front claws.

Dryosaurus

The fossils of this ornithopod, of the suborder Ornithischia, were found in Tanzania and the United States at the same time during the 19th century, in the middle of the so-called "Bone Wars." This lightweight herbivore could reach up to 14.8 feet (4.5 m) long and weigh nearly 200 pounds (90 kg).

CAMARASAURUS
means "chambered lizard."

Camarasaurus

This large, herbivorous sauropod lived on the plains of North America 159 million years ago. Its fossils were first found in 1877. It grew up to 65.5 feet (20 m) long; even so, it was easy prey for large predators such as Allosaurus. It could weigh up to 22 tons (20 metric tons), and it walked on four feet, which prevented it from running quickly enough to easily escape.

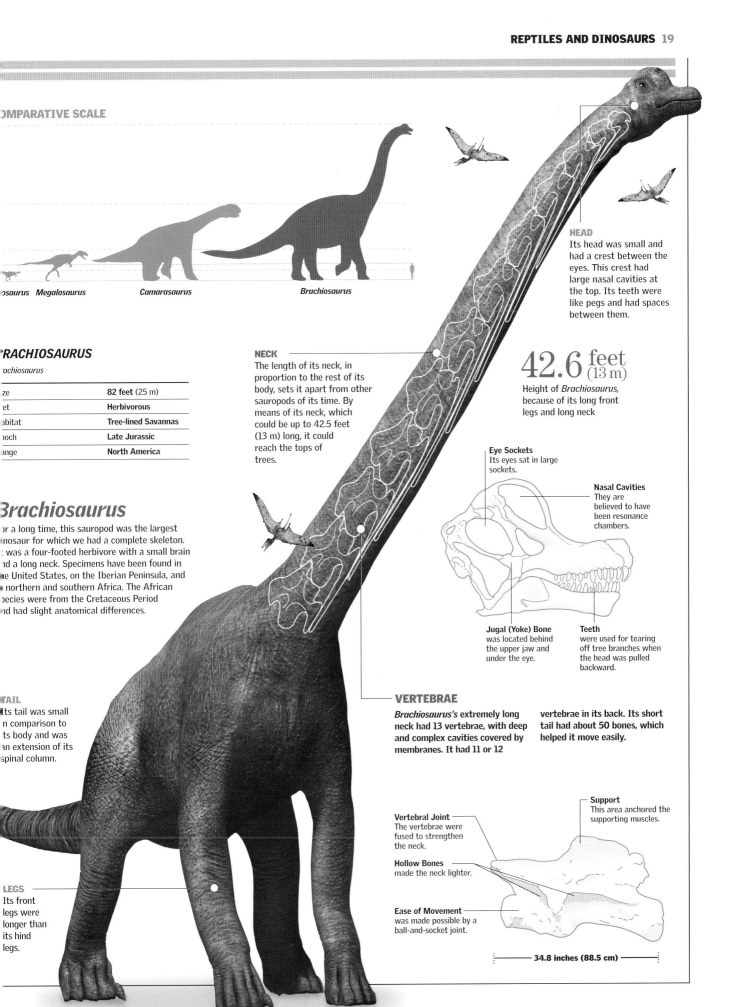

MPARATIVE SCALE

saurus Megalosaurus   Camarasaurus   Brachiosaurus

RACHIOSAURUS

achiosaurus

ze	**82 feet (25 m)**
et	**Herbivorous**
abitat	**Tree-lined Savannas**
och	**Late Jurassic**
ange	**North America**

Brachiosaurus

or a long time, this sauropod was the largest
inosaur for which we had a complete skeleton.
: was a four-footed herbivore with a small brain
nd a long neck. Specimens have been found in
e United States, on the Iberian Peninsula, and
northern and southern Africa. The African
ecies were from the Cretaceous Period
nd had slight anatomical differences.

TAIL
ts tail was small
n comparison to
ts body and was
an extension of its
spinal column.

LEGS
Its front
legs were
longer than
its hind
legs.

NECK
The length of its neck, in
proportion to the rest of its
body, sets it apart from other
sauropods of its time. By
means of its neck, which
could be up to 42.5 feet
(13 m) long, it could
reach the tops of
trees.

HEAD
Its head was small and
had a crest between the
eyes. This crest had
large nasal cavities at
the top. Its teeth were
like pegs and had spaces
between them.

42.6 feet (13 m)
Height of *Brachiosaurus*,
because of its long front
legs and long neck

Eye Sockets
Its eyes sat in large
sockets.

Nasal Cavities
They are
believed to have
been resonance
chambers.

Jugal (Yoke) Bone
was located behind
the upper jaw and
under the eye.

Teeth
were used for tearing
off tree branches when
the head was pulled
backward.

VERTEBRAE
Brachiosaurus's extremely long
neck had 13 vertebrae, with deep
and complex cavities covered by
membranes. It had 11 or 12
vertebrae in its back. Its short
tail had about 50 bones, which
helped it move easily.

Vertebral Joint
The vertebrae were
fused to strengthen
the neck.

Hollow Bones
made the neck lighter.

Ease of Movement
was made possible by a
ball-and-socket joint.

Support
This area anchored the
supporting muscles.

34.8 inches (88.5 cm)

A Docile Vegetarian

This striking dinosaur is one of the most widely studied in the history of paleontology. The first fossils were discovered by Othniel C. Marsh in 1877 in the American West, during the "Bone Wars." This quadruped herbivore could measure up to 29.5 feet (9 m) long and weigh up to 2.2 tons (2 metric tons). Because of its small head, it has been used since the 19th century as a symbol of stupidity. It was later shown that most dinosaurs had small brains and that *Stegosaurus*'s brain was larger than average.

Head
Its lightweight head had small teeth that were of little use for chewing, so it swallowed plants whole.

Legs
Its front legs were half as long as its hind legs. Each foot had five wide, short toes.

Stegosaurus

was an ornithischian dinosaur that belonged to the family Stegosauridae. Its distinctive features included wide plates on its back and four spines, up to 24 inches (60 cm) long, on its tail. The function of these features is still under debate, but it is believed that they served mainly for self-defense.

Stegosaurus was an easy victim for the great predators of its time, such as *Allosaurus*, but it is also believed that it may have been hunted by packs of small predators, such as *Ornitholestes*. It is doubtful that *Stegosaurus* could raise itself up on its hind legs, so it probably fed mostly on low bushes.

STEGOSAURUS

Stegosaurus armatus

Size	29.5 feet (9 m)
Diet	Herbivorous
Habitat	Subtropical Forests
Epoch	Late Jurassic
Range	North America

WHERE IT LIVED
The first fossils were found in Colorado. Other specimens have since been found in India, western Europe, southern Africa, and China.

Tail
Stegosaurus's only real defense was likely the four spines on its tail, which it swung back and forth.

PLATES
These triangular bony structures were not very solid, but they had a complex network of veins. The plates were likely used to regulate the animal's body temperature or even for courtship.

Dorsal Plate   Caudal Plate   Cervical Plate

The Cretaceous Period

W as an age of expansion. The dinosaurs continued to diversify, and the first snakes appeared. The Earth began to look like the planet we know today. The movement of tectonic plates created folds that came to form some of the mountain ranges of today, such as the Appalachians in North America and the Alps in Europe. At the end of this period, another mass extinction event occurred, probably caused by the impact of a meteorite.●

CRETACEOUS
The name is based on the Latin word *creta*, which means stone. The name comes from the layer of limestone found in the rock formations that define this geological system.

FORESTS
Oaks and maples predominated in the most humid regions.

Flora

During the early Cretaceous Period, ferns and conifers predominated. Important groups became extinct at the boundary between the Early and Late Cretaceous. These species were replaced in tropical forest environments by flowering plants, which spread to colder and drier areas.

FLOWERS
During this period, the main advancement in the evolution of plants was the appearance of angiosperms, or plants with flowers and fruit.

An Evolving Planet

During this period of 80 million years, the Earth's climate changed. Its temperate climate, accompanied by snow in the polar regions during the winter, was transformed into a warm, mild climate with noticeably different seasons. The ocean levels rose, currents increased ocean temperatures, and marine fauna multiplied. On land, the first flowering plants (gymnosperms) appeared, and forests of willow, maple, and oak harbored the last large dinosaurs.

ALPINE MOUNTAIN-BUILDING
During this period, Africa and Eurasia drifted closer together. The Tethys Sea narrowed, and the collision of plates formed the Alpine mountain range.

140 TO 65

MILLION YEARS AGO
The Earth began to adopt an appearance similar to that of today. Africa and South America separated from one another, as did North America and Europe. The North and South American plates drifted westward and collided with the Pacific plate, raising both the Rocky Mountains in North America and the Andes in South America.

NORTH AMERICA
EURASIA
SOUTH AMERICA
AFRICA
INDIA
ANTARCTICA

FLYING REPTILES
developed very large wingspans toward the end of this period.

MARINE REPTILES
The expanding seas caused an abundance of marine reptiles and other aquatic species, such as mollusks.

Fauna

The Cretaceous Period held the greatest diversity of dinosaurs. This epoch is also known for small mammals, insects, and the largest flying reptiles.

A Fierce Era

T he Cretaceous Period saw both the splendor and the end of the "Age of Reptiles." It was the longest period of the Mesozoic Era, and for 80 million years, specific types of animal life developed in each region. South America was home to the largest herbivore known, *Argentinosaurus huinculensis*, which lived at the same time as the fearsome theropods. Some species of this period later survived the mass extinction—especially marine invertebrates, such as crustaceans, gastropod mollusks, and advanced ray-finned fish. Small mammals such as *Zalambdalestes* also survived. ●

The Struggle to Survive

Dinosaurs remained dominant during the Cretaceous Period. Although the large sauropods still existed, new groups emerged, intensifying the competition for resources. Enormous carnivores of the tyrannosaur family in North America and the giganotosaurs in South America were the largest threats to the peaceful herbivores. New, distinctive species, such as the duck-billed hadrosaurs and the armored *Triceratops*, also appeared.

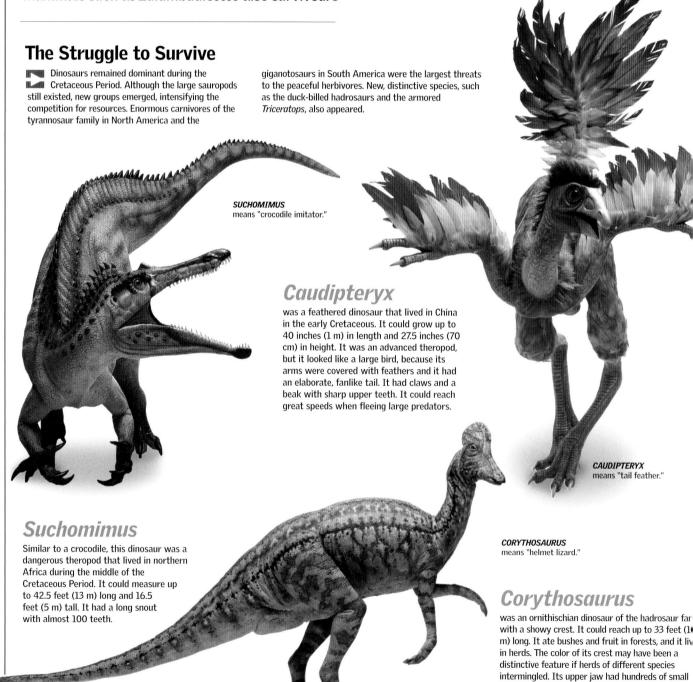

SUCHOMIMUS
means "crocodile imitator."

Caudipteryx

was a feathered dinosaur that lived in China in the early Cretaceous. It could grow up to 40 inches (1 m) in length and 27.5 inches (70 cm) in height. It was an advanced theropod, but it looked like a large bird, because its arms were covered with feathers and it had an elaborate, fanlike tail. It had claws and a beak with sharp upper teeth. It could reach great speeds when fleeing large predators.

CAUDIPTERYX
means "tail feather."

CORYTHOSAURUS
means "helmet lizard."

Suchomimus

Similar to a crocodile, this dinosaur was a dangerous theropod that lived in northern Africa during the middle of the Cretaceous Period. It could measure up to 42.5 feet (13 m) long and 16.5 feet (5 m) tall. It had a long snout with almost 100 teeth.

Corythosaurus

was an ornithischian dinosaur of the hadrosaur far with a showy crest. It could reach up to 33 feet (1 m) long. It ate bushes and fruit in forests, and it liv in herds. The color of its crest may have been a distinctive feature if herds of different species intermingled. Its upper jaw had hundreds of small teeth that were replaced often.

Therizinosaurus

Some scientists believe that this mysterious dinosaur was herbivorous. However, it has been classified as a theropod that lived during the Late Cretaceous in the region of the Gobi Desert in Mongolia. It was first identified in 1954, and its name means "scythe lizard." It was between 26 and 39.5 feet (8-12 m) long and weighed about 5 tons (4.5 metric tons). It was believed to have possessed a lifestyle similar to modern gorillas or the extinct giant ground sloths.

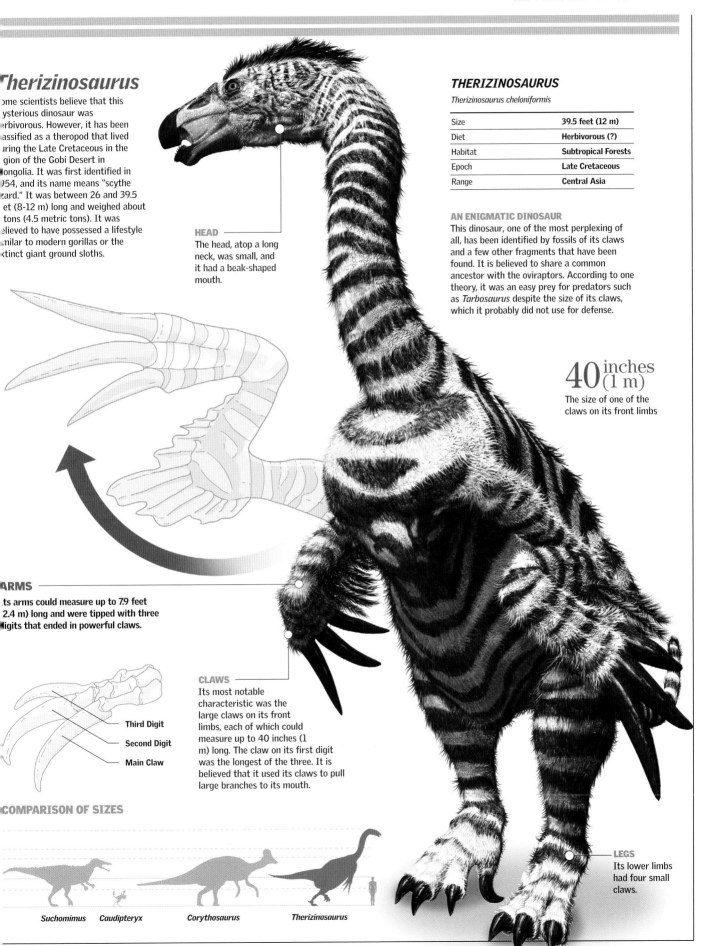

HEAD
The head, atop a long neck, was small, and it had a beak-shaped mouth.

THERIZINOSAURUS

Therizinosaurus cheloniformis

Size	39.5 feet (12 m)
Diet	Herbivorous (?)
Habitat	Subtropical Forests
Epoch	Late Cretaceous
Range	Central Asia

AN ENIGMATIC DINOSAUR
This dinosaur, one of the most perplexing of all, has been identified by fossils of its claws and a few other fragments that have been found. It is believed to share a common ancestor with the oviraptors. According to one theory, it was an easy prey for predators such as *Tarbosaurus* despite the size of its claws, which it probably did not use for defense.

40 inches (1 m)
The size of one of the claws on its front limbs

ARMS
Its arms could measure up to 7.9 feet (2.4 m) long and were tipped with three digits that ended in powerful claws.

Third Digit
Second Digit
Main Claw

CLAWS
Its most notable characteristic was the large claws on its front limbs, each of which could measure up to 40 inches (1 m) long. The claw on its first digit was the longest of the three. It is believed that it used its claws to pull large branches to its mouth.

COMPARISON OF SIZES

Suchomimus   Caudipteryx   Corythosaurus   Therizinosaurus

LEGS
Its lower limbs had four small claws.

The Great Predator of the Sout

he largest carnivorous dinosaur that has ever existed on Earth lived 95 million years ago during the Late Cretaceous Period. Fossils of *Giganotosaurus carolinii* were first found by Rubén Carolini, a mechanic and amateur paleontologist, in 1993. The name means "giant southern lizard." Although only 70 percent of its skeleton was found, it is known that it could reach a length of up to 49 feet (15 m) and that it hunted large sauropods.

Giganotosaurus carolinii

➤ belonged to the order Saurischia, the suborder Theropoda, and the superfamily Allosauridae. It could measure up to 16.5 feet (5 m) in height and weigh 8.8 tons (8 metric tons). The fossilized bones that have been found for this dinosaur include the skull, pelvis, femur, spinal column, and upper limbs. It was thought to hunt in packs, because several fossils have been found together. This made it a deadly threat to the large, herbivorous sauropods of the time.

Powerful Jaws

All predators in the superfamily Allosauridae had powerful jaws and rounded teeth with serrated edges to tear the flesh of their victims. Each tooth could be up to 8 inches (20 cm) long.

1 Movable Skull
Its skull slid over its lower jaw so that its knifelike teeth could cut.

2 Lateral Expansion
The joints of its skull bones moved outward to better grip its victim.

Large Head

Its head was very large in relation to its body, measuring up to 5.9 feet (1.8 m) long.

Claws

Both the hind legs and the front legs had three toes. The front limbs had sharp claws.

A New King

For a time, *Tyrannosaurus rex* was considered the largest land predator, although it is now believed by some to have been a scavenger. In 1997, a larger and more fearsome predator was made known to the scientific community. *Giganotosaurus* is considered by some to be the king of the dinosaurs.

GIGANOTOSAURUS
Giganotosaurus carolinii

Size	49 feet (15 m) long
Diet	Carnivorous
Habitat	Forests and Wetlands
Epoch	Late Cretaceous
Range	South America

WHERE IT LIVED

The fossils of this giant predator were found in the province of Neuquén in the region of Patagonia in Argentina.

Tail
Filled with solid vertebrae, it was used to maintain balance and could probably swing from side to side.

Swift Hunter
Giganotosaurus's well-developed hind legs enabled it to run at high speed while hunting its prey.

Living Life to the Limit

Extinctions of living beings on Earth have occurred in a series of drastic episodes throughout history, from the Cambrian Period to the Cretaceous. The most famous chapter is associated with the total disappearance of the dinosaurs about 65.5 million years ago. This mass extinction of these large reptiles is so important that it was used by scientists to indicate the end of the Cretaceous Period and the beginning of the Tertiary, a designation known as the K-T boundary ("K" is the abbreviation for Cretaceous). Natural phenomena of terrestrial or extraterrestrial origin are possible causes of the disappearance of these gigantic animals of the Mesozoic Era. ●

Fatal Meteorites

1 In its long geological history, the Earth has witnessed several mass extinctions. Some scientists argue that the cause could be the same in all cases, and they point to extraterrestrial phenomena as the most likely cause. However, this hypothesis has been widely criticized. From the Paleozoic Era 570 million years ago to the Cretaceous Period, it has been determined that there were five or six mass extinctions on Earth, which mark the boundaries between the following periods: Cambrian-Ordovician, Ordovician-Silurian, Devonian-Carboniferous, and Permian-Cretaceous. However, scientists have yet to determine a convincing factor that could be the cause in all cases. The Devonian extinction exterminated 50 percent of all species, much like the one occurring at the K-T boundary. However, the largest extinction of all occurred in the Permian Period, in which 95 percent of all species were eliminated.

CLUES IN CHICXULUB

In the town of Chicxulub, on the Yucatán Peninsula in Mexico, a depression was found that measured 112 miles (180 km) across. This enormous imprint was evidence of the violent impact of an extremely large meteorite that crashed into the Earth.

MIXED ROCKS
Samples taken from the Chicxulub crater show a mixture of terrestrial minerals (dark areas) and meteorite minerals (light areas).

POST-EXTINCTION LAYER
Sediments of microfossils from eras later than that of the dinosaurs

FIREBALL LAYER
Dust and ash from the meteorite's impact

EJECTION LAYER
Materials from the crater that settled during several months

PRE-EXTINCTION LAYER
Sediments with microfossils from the era of the dinosaurs

50% OF ALL SPECIES became extinct at the K-T boundary.

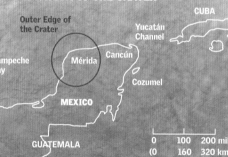

LOCATION OF THE CRATER

Outer Edge of the Crater

Campeche Bay

Mérida

Cancún

Yucatán Channel

CUBA

Cozumel

MEXICO

GUATEMALA

0	100	200 miles
(0	160	320 km)

Other Proposed Theories

Not all scientists agree with the idea that a large meteorite caused the mass extinction of the dinosaurs. Rather, they suggest that the Chicxulub crater was formed 300,000 years before the end of the Cretaceous Period. These scientists claim that terrestrial events, such as volcanic eruptions, were more likely to have caused the Cretaceous extinction. According to intermediate positions, the eruptions may have been caused by a large meteorite impact.

② FROM HERE...

During the Cretaceous Period, intense volcanic activity on Earth caused frequent, copious eruptions of lava and ash that exterminated the dinosaurs. Over 386 square miles (1,000 sq km) of volcanic rock deposited on the Deccan Plateau in India lend credence to this scientific hypothesis of the Cretaceous extinction.

③ ...OR FROM THERE

As the Solar System crosses the galactic plane of the Milky Way, every 67 million years it changes the paths of meteoroids and comets in the Oort cloud. These bodies could enter the inner Solar System as meteors and possibly strike the Earth as meteorites.

6 miles (10 km)

DIAMETER OF THE ASTEROID that caused the Chicxulub crater in Mexico

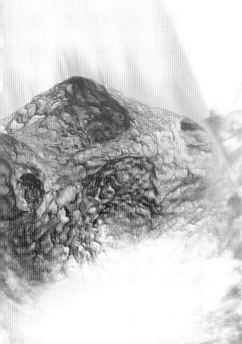

50 million

ATOMIC BOMBS like the one dropped on Hiroshima equal the force of the impact of one meteorite measuring 6 miles (10 km) in diameter.

112 miles (180 km)

DIAMETER OF THE CHICXULUB CRATER on the Yucatán Peninsula

Reptiles: Background

olor plays a very important role in the life of iguanas and lizards. It helps to differentiate males and females, and when it is time to attract a mate, the members of the iguana family communicate by showing bright colors, tufts of feathers, and folds of skin. Another particularity that distinguishes iguanas is their coverir of epidermal scales. In addition, like all

GOOD VISION
Iguanas have very good
vision. They see colors, and
they have transparent eyelids
that close easily.

...eptiles, they are not capable of generating
...nternal heat, so they depend on external
...actors to maintain their body temperature.
...'or this reason, you will frequently see
...guanas lying stretched out in the sun.

When it comes to their diet, most reptiles
are carnivores, with the exception of some
turtles, which are herbivores. Reptiles are
also characterized by their total
independence from aquatic environments.●

A Skin with Scales

Reptiles are vertebrates, meaning that they are animals with a spinal column. Their skin is hard, dry, and flaky. Like birds, most reptiles are born from eggs deposited on land. The offspring hatch fully formed without passing through a larval stage. The first reptiles appeared during the height of the Carboniferous Period in the Paleozoic Era. During the Mesozoic Era, they evolved and flourished, which is why this period is also known as the age of reptiles. Only 5 of the 23 orders that existed then have living representatives today. ●

SOLOMON ISLAND SKINK
Corucia zebrata

EMBRIONARY MEMBRANES
They develop two: a protective amnion and a respiratory allantoid (or fetal vascular) membrane.

EYES
are almost always small. In diurnal animals, the pupil is rounded.

NICTITATING MEMBRANE
extends forward from the internal angle of the eye and covers it.

4,765
SPECIES OF LIZARDS EXIST.

Habitat

Reptiles have a great capacity to adapt, since they can occupy an incredible variety of environments. They live on every continent except Antarctica, and most countries have at least one species of terrestrial reptile. They can be found in the driest and hottest deserts, as well as the steamiest, most humid rainforests. They are especially common in the tropical and subtropical regions of Africa, Asia, Australia, and the Americas, where high temperatures and a great diversity of prey allow them to thrive.

BLACK CAIMAN
Melanosuchus niger

Crocodiles

are distinguished by their usually large size. From neck to tail, their backs are covered in rows of bony plates, which can give the impression of thorns or teeth. Crocodiles appeared toward the end of the Triassic Period, and they are the closest living relatives to both dinosaurs and birds. Their hearts are divided into four chambers, their brains show a high degree of development, and the musculature of their abdomens is so developed that it resembles the gizzards of birds. The larger species are very dangerous.

OVIPAROUS
Most reptiles are oviparous (they lay eggs); however, many species of snakes and lizards are ovoviviparous (they give birth to live offspring).

THORAX AND ABDOMEN
are not separated by a diaphragm. Alligators breathe with the help of muscles on the walls of their body.

AMERICAN ALLIGATOR
Alligator mississippiensis

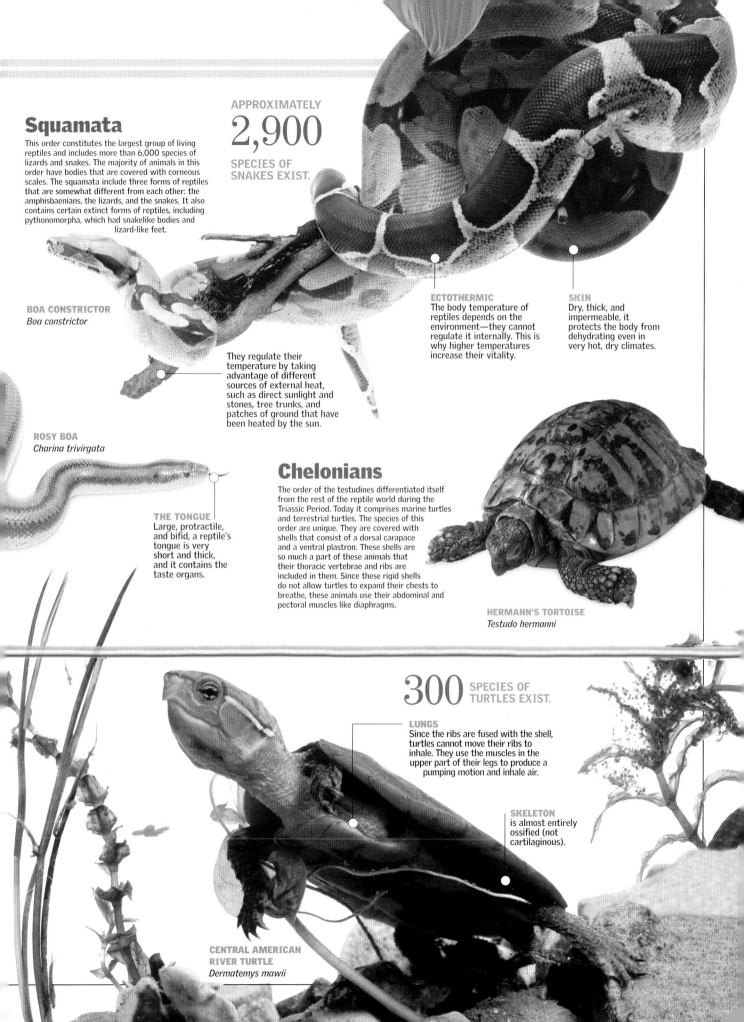

Squamata

This order constitutes the largest group of living reptiles and includes more than 6,000 species of lizards and snakes. The majority of animals in this order have bodies that are covered with corneous scales. The squamata include three forms of reptiles that are somewhat different from each other: the amphisbaenians, the lizards, and the snakes. It also contains certain extinct forms of reptiles, including pythonomorpha, which had snakelike bodies and lizard-like feet.

APPROXIMATELY
2,900
SPECIES OF
SNAKES EXIST.

BOA CONSTRICTOR
Boa constrictor

They regulate their temperature by taking advantage of different sources of external heat, such as direct sunlight and stones, tree trunks, and patches of ground that have been heated by the sun.

ECTOTHERMIC
The body temperature of reptiles depends on the environment—they cannot regulate it internally. This is why higher temperatures increase their vitality.

SKIN
Dry, thick, and impermeable, it protects the body from dehydrating even in very hot, dry climates.

ROSY BOA
Charina trivirgata

THE TONGUE
Large, protractile, and bifid, a reptile's tongue is very short and thick, and it contains the taste organs.

Chelonians

The order of the testudines differentiated itself from the rest of the reptile world during the Triassic Period. Today it comprises marine turtles and terrestrial turtles. The species of this order are unique. They are covered with shells that consist of a dorsal carapace and a ventral plastron. These shells are so much a part of these animals that their thoracic vertebrae and ribs are included in them. Since these rigid shells do not allow turtles to expand their chests to breathe, these animals use their abdominal and pectoral muscles like diaphragms.

HERMANN'S TORTOISE
Testudo hermanni

300 SPECIES OF TURTLES EXIST.

LUNGS
Since the ribs are fused with the shell, turtles cannot move their ribs to inhale. They use the muscles in the upper part of their legs to produce a pumping motion and inhale air.

SKELETON
is almost entirely ossified (not cartilaginous).

CENTRAL AMERICAN RIVER TURTLE
Dermatemys mawii

The Family Tree

The first reptiles descended from ancestral amphibians. They distinguished themselves from their ancestors through mutations that allowed them to free themselves from their dependence on water for reproduction. Among these adaptations, the amniotic egg stands out, but equally important were the development of sex organs that favored internal copulation, an impermeable skin, and the formation of a low volume of urine that eliminates uric acid instead of urea. These adaptations to its environment were necessary to the reptilian dominance of the greater part of the Mesozoic Era. ●

REPTILE EVOLUTION

Ichthyosaurs

Marine Reptiles

Lizards

Metriorhynchus

CROCODILIANS

SAUROPTERYGIANS

Scutosaurus

Hylonomus

CAPTORHINIDS AND *HYLONOMUS*

Snakes, Lizards, and Sphenodonts

ARCHOSAURUS Antorbital fenestra

Archelon

Diapsid skull

ANAPSIDS

Canine teeth in the upper mandible

REPTILES

TEETH
Small and irregular, they allowed the animal to cut buds for food.

FEET
were appropriate for the animal's body weight. It moved slowly.

SHELL
was a structure formed by bony ribs that developed from the vertebrae of the spine.

Great Turtle

The *Archelon ischyros* was a giant marine reptile that measured 15 feet (4.6 m) in length. It inhabited North America during the Upper Cretaceous (between 75 and 65 million years ago). An omnivorous feeder, it passed slowly through shallow waters by means of the propulsion provided by its flippers. The females laid eggs in holes just like the sea turtles of today.

Weight
4,900 pounds
(2,200 kg)

15 feet (4.6 m)

ARCHELON

Scientific Name	*Archelon ischyro*
Diet	Omnivorous
Habitat	Marine
Location	North America
Era	Upper Cretaceou

GIANT FLIPPERS
were used to move through the water.

MOUTH
had a beak like a hook. It did not cut, but its bite was deadly.

4,900 pounds (2,200 kg)
IS WHAT THESE SEA TURTLES COULD HAVE WEIGHED.

Tough Skin

ARMOR
Sharp points formed a protective armor against predators.

Scutosaurs were quadrupeds with massive legs, similar to strong columns with wide bases, which sustained the weight of their bodies. These reptiles belonged to the extinct genus *Scutosaurus* species. They were large herbivores that lumbered through the pines and firs of Permian forests in search of food, such as herbs and soft buds.

Weight 1,100 pounds (500 kg)

8 feet (2.5 m)

SHIELD LIZARD

Scientific Name	*Scutosaurus* sp.
Diet	Herbivore
Habitat	Land
Location	Europe (Russia)
Era	End of Permian

TAIL
was short in relation to the animal's body size.

5 **ORDERS OF REPTILES EXIST TODAY.**

FLIPPERS
maintained the body's balance while it moved.

SKIN
was smooth and slippery.

JAW
was thin and pronounced, with small and sharp teeth.

160 **MILLION YEARS IS THE AGE OF THE MOST PRIMITIVE SEA CROCODILE FOSSIL.**

Sea Crocodiles

This genus of reptiles owes its name to its members' long snouts. The sea crocodile was a dangerous hunter, capable and opportunistic. It preyed on squid and pterosaurs, and it chased fish up to 20 feet (6 m) long—twice its own size. Its tail got thinner toward its end, which had a flipper. There was a small bump between its eyes. Sea crocodiles lived near the end of the Jurassic Period.

Skull Types

The fossils of the most primitive reptiles correspond with the Lower Carboniferous Period. These reptiles were terrestrial animals, somewhat similar to the Mesozoic reptiles. The diapsid lineage originated with them.

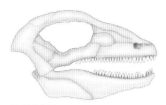

ANAPSID
A group of reptiles without openings in the skull near the temples. This is the condition seen in fish, amphibians, and earlier reptiles. Today's turtles belong to this lineage.

Cranial Opening

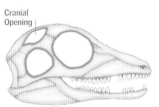

DIAPSID
During the Permian Period, another group of reptiles emerged that had temporal openings in the skull behind each eye socket.

TAIL
was very flexible, and it provided great agility for swimming.

Weight 660 pounds (300 kg)
10 feet (3 m)

METRYORHYNCHUS

Scientific Name	*Metriorhynchus* sp.
Diet	Squid and Pterosaurs
Habitat	Marine
Location	South America (Chile) and Europe (France and England)
Era	Jurassic

A Living Fossil

D espite looking like lizards and sharing some common traits with crocodiles, tuataras are a unique type of reptile. The tuatara is the last living sphenodont, and, because it has changed very little from its original form, it is called a living fossil. Two known species of tuatara have been identified, both of which inhabit the islands that lie off the coast of New Zealand. They live in burrows, and their great tolerance for cold allows them to survive at very low temperatures. Tuataras grow slowly and can live up to 80 years. ●

TUATARA
Sphenodon punctatus

Habitat	**Stephens Island**
Reproduction	**Oviparous**
Lifestyle	**Burrower**

The males are much larger than the females.

Weight
25 ounces (700 g)

┌─ **Average Length: 16 to 24 inches** ─┐
(40 to 60 cm)

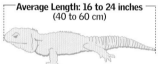

PINEAL EYE
can be distinguished in younger specimens. In adults, it is covered by the scales that grow over it.

SPINES
These smooth and conspicuous spines are more prominent in males.

HEAD
is large compared to the body, and it lacks auditory structures.

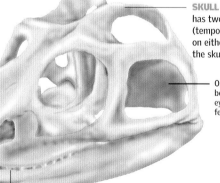

SKULL
has two openings (temporal fenestra) on either side of the skull.

Openings behind each eye (temporal fenestra)

EYE
is large. The pupil is a vertical slit, and the iris is a dark brown color.

COLORATION
Tuataras' tones vary from grayish to olive to brick red. Tuataras undergo significant variations in color throughout their lives.

TEETH
are not separated structures but rather a sharpened extension of the edges of both jaws.

NUTRITION
Tuataras are carnivores. Their diet consists of insects, earthworms, snails, and crickets. Occasionally they eat shearwater eggs and nestlings.

150 million years

THE LENGTH OF TIME TUATARAS HAVE EXISTED WITHOUT UNDERGOING EVOLUTIONARY CHANGES.

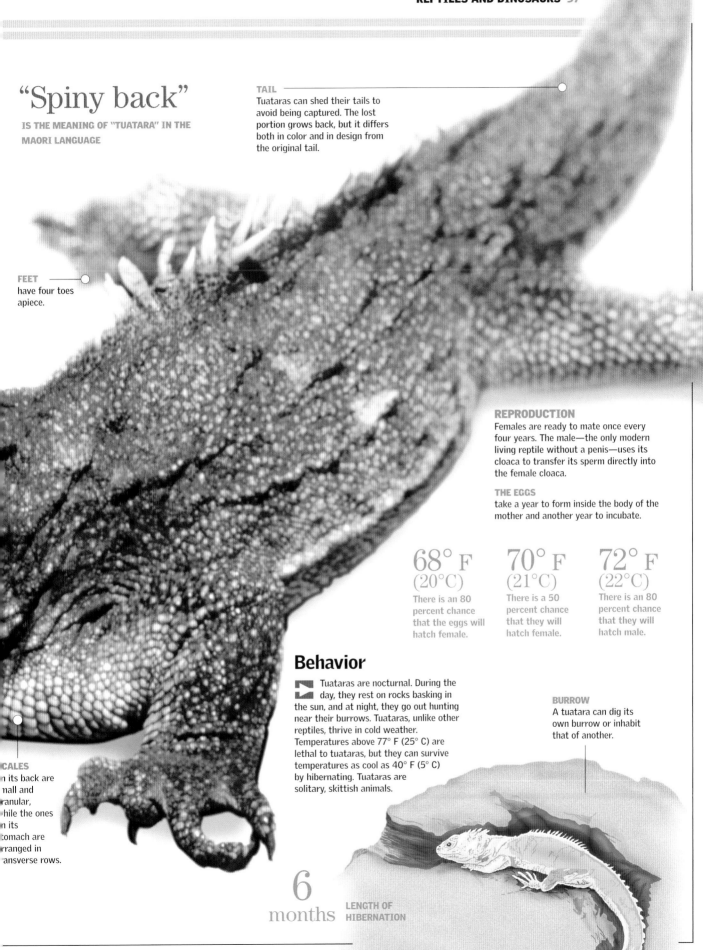

"Spiny back"

IS THE MEANING OF "TUATARA" IN THE MAORI LANGUAGE

TAIL
Tuataras can shed their tails to avoid being captured. The lost portion grows back, but it differs both in color and in design from the original tail.

FEET
have four toes apiece.

CALES
n its back are
nall and
ranular,
while the ones
n its
tomach are
rranged in
ransverse rows.

REPRODUCTION
Females are ready to mate once every four years. The male—the only modern living reptile without a penis—uses its cloaca to transfer its sperm directly into the female cloaca.

THE EGGS
take a year to form inside the body of the mother and another year to incubate.

68° F
(20°C)
There is an 80 percent chance that the eggs will hatch female.

70° F
(21°C)
There is a 50 percent chance that they will hatch female.

72° F
(22°C)
There is an 80 percent chance that they will hatch male.

Behavior

Tuataras are nocturnal. During the day, they rest on rocks basking in the sun, and at night, they go out hunting near their burrows. Tuataras, unlike other reptiles, thrive in cold weather. Temperatures above 77° F (25° C) are lethal to tuataras, but they can survive temperatures as cool as 40° F (5° C) by hibernating. Tuataras are solitary, skittish animals.

BURROW
A tuatara can dig its own burrow or inhabit that of another.

6
months
LENGTH OF HIBERNATION

Internal Organs

The anatomy of reptiles enables them to live on land. Thanks to their dry, scaly skin and their excretion of uric acid instead of urea, they minimize water loss. The heart distributes blood in a double circuit. Crocodiles were the first vertebrates to have a four-chambered heart; the separation of the ventricles is incomplete in all other reptiles. The lungs, developed beyond those of amphibians, contribute to cardiac efficiency by allowing for greater exchange of gases. ●

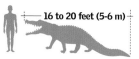

16 to 20 feet (5-6 m)

Weight: more than 1 ton

NILE CROCODILE
Crocodylus niloticus

Diet	Carnivorous
Longevity	45 years in the wild and 80 years in captivity

SKIN
Reptiles have chromatophores that modify their color to a small degree. Two unique traits of crocodiles are that the skin on the head has glands that regulate the body's ionic balance, and the cloaca has glands that secrete substances crucial for mating and defense.

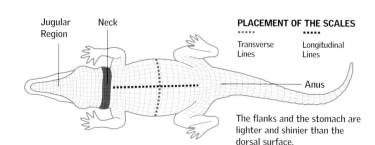

Jugular Region | Neck

PLACEMENT OF THE SCALES

Transverse Lines | Longitudinal Lines

Anus

The flanks and the stomach are lighter and shinier than the dorsal surface.

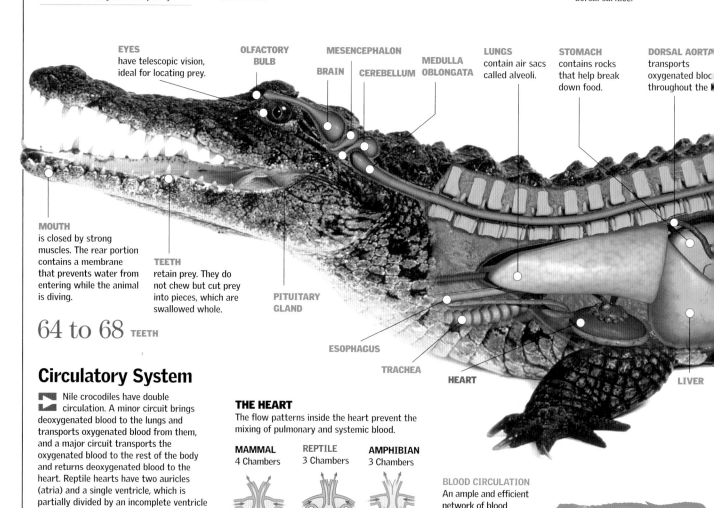

EYES
have telescopic vision, ideal for locating prey.

OLFACTORY BULB

BRAIN

MESENCEPHALON

CEREBELLUM

MEDULLA OBLONGATA

LUNGS
contain air sacs called alveoli.

STOMACH
contains rocks that help break down food.

DORSAL AORTA
transports oxygenated blood throughout the

MOUTH
is closed by strong muscles. The rear portion contains a membrane that prevents water from entering while the animal is diving.

TEETH
retain prey. They do not chew but cut prey into pieces, which are swallowed whole.

PITUITARY GLAND

ESOPHAGUS

TRACHEA

HEART

LIVER

64 to 68 TEETH

Circulatory System

▶ Nile crocodiles have double circulation. A minor circuit brings deoxygenated blood to the lungs and transports oxygenated blood from them, and a major circuit transports the oxygenated blood to the rest of the body and returns deoxygenated blood to the heart. Reptile hearts have two auricles (atria) and a single ventricle, which is partially divided by an incomplete ventricle partition.

THE HEART
The flow patterns inside the heart prevent the mixing of pulmonary and systemic blood.

MAMMAL
4 Chambers

REPTILE
3 Chambers

AMPHIBIAN
3 Chambers

BLOOD CIRCULATION
An ample and efficient network of blood vessels extends throughout the bodies of reptiles.

A Question of Skin

The absence of extremities and the friction produced during movement give snakes the ability to slide and to shed their skin in one motion. Other reptiles must shed their skin by tearing it off in pieces. Reptiles shed their skin regularly and continue to do so even in the last years of their lives.

CORAL SNAKE
Micrurus altirostris
It is characterized by its smooth and brightly colored scales.

NEW SKIN
is smooth and bright.

OLD SKIN
is fragile. It rips easily.

100
THE NUMBER OF TIMES A VIPER SHEDS ITS SKIN OVER ITS LIFETIME.

Melanophores

Osteoderms

Flexible Joint

GROWTH OF THE SCALES

Epidermis

Dermis

1 The dermal layer is found below the epidermis.

2 Differentiation takes place during dermal cell growth.

3 The epidermis secretes large amounts of keratin.

4 The new scales overlap each other and cover the skin.

SPLEEN

TESTICLES
Lobuled. Their ducts empty in the cloaca.

KIDNEYS
Metanephric. The ureters empty in the cloaca.

DOUBLE CAUDAL CREST

CLOACA
Shared opening of the excretory, reproductive, and digestive ducts

SIMPLE CAUDAL CREST

SMALL INTESTINE

COLON

Respiratory System

is completely pulmonary. Most reptiles possess a pair of functional lungs, with the exception of snakes, which have only one functional lung. Body-wall muscles generate the pressure differences necessary to circulate air through the airways from the nasal cavities to the pulmonary alveoli.

BREATHING

1 **EXHALING**
Internal organs are compressed. This, in turn, compresses the lungs and causes them to expel air.

2 **INHALING**
The pelvic bones rotate downward, the abdomen stretches, and the muscles cause the lungs to expand.

Abdominal Muscles

The liver compresses the lungs.

Air is expelled.

The pressure difference causes the lungs to expand and take in air.

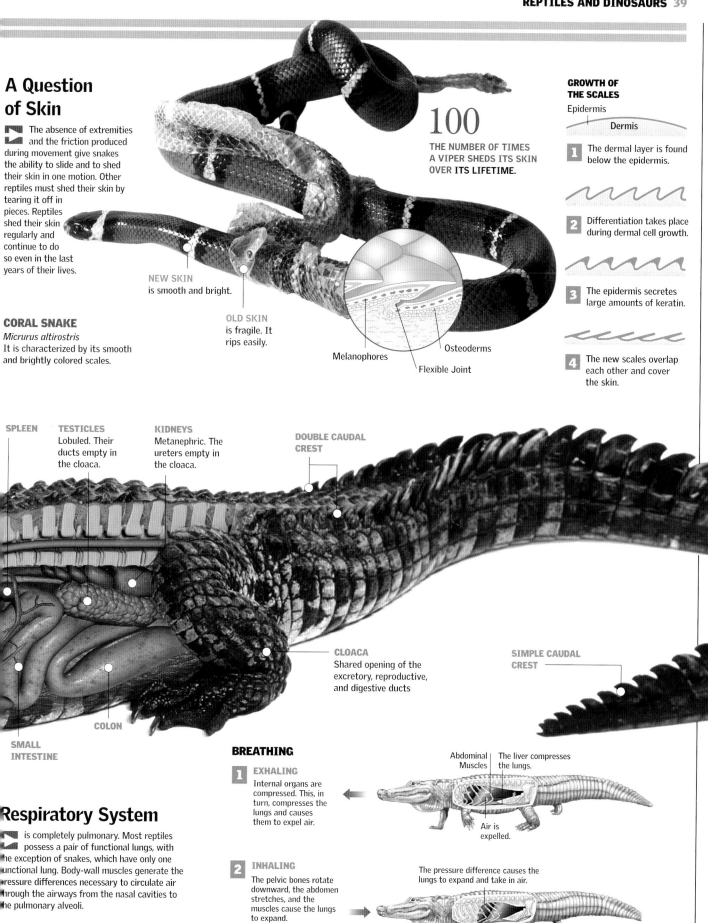

A Menu at Ground Level

R eptiles are basically carnivorous, even though some follow other food regimens. Lizards usually feed on insects. Snakes usually feed on small vertebrates like birds, rodents, fish, amphibians, or even other reptiles. For many, the eggs of birds and other reptiles make a very succulent meal. The painted turtle is omnivorous: it eats meat and plants. Reptiles and other species are part of a larger food chain—animals eat other animals, preserving the equilibrium of the environment. ●

Herbivores

This diet is generally typical of other groups of animals; however, there are reptiles that feed only on green leaves and plants. The marine iguana eats only the algae that it finds under rocks on the sea floor.

GREEN IGUANA
Also called the common iguana, it is one of the few herbivorous reptiles. It feeds on green leaves as well as on some fruits.

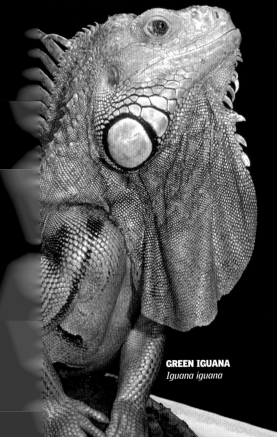

GREEN IGUANA
Iguana iguana

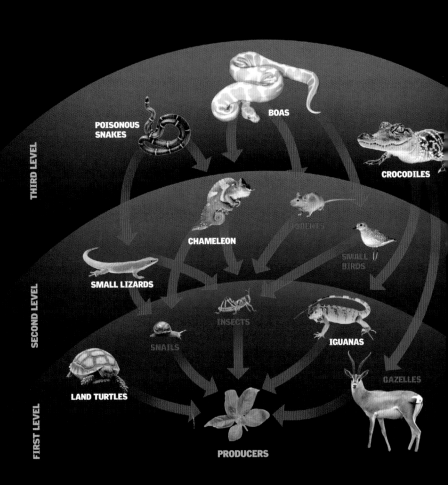

POISONOUS SNAKES

BOAS

CROCODILES

THIRD LEVEL

CHAMELEON

RODENTS

SMALL BIRDS

SMALL LIZARDS

SECOND LEVEL

INSECTS

IGUANAS

SNAILS

GAZELLES

FIRST LEVEL

LAND TURTLES

PRODUCERS

The Food Chain

Because they use photosynthesis, which permits inorganic carbon to be transformed into organic material, plants are the only true "producers" in the food chain. Herbivores feed on them and are thus first-level consumers. The animals that feed on the herbivores are second-level consumers, and the animals that eat other carnivores—a category that includes some reptiles—form the third level of consumers in the food chain.

Metabolism

In the case of snakes that swallow their prey whole, digestion takes weeks and sometimes even months. Their gastric juices digest even the bones of their prey.

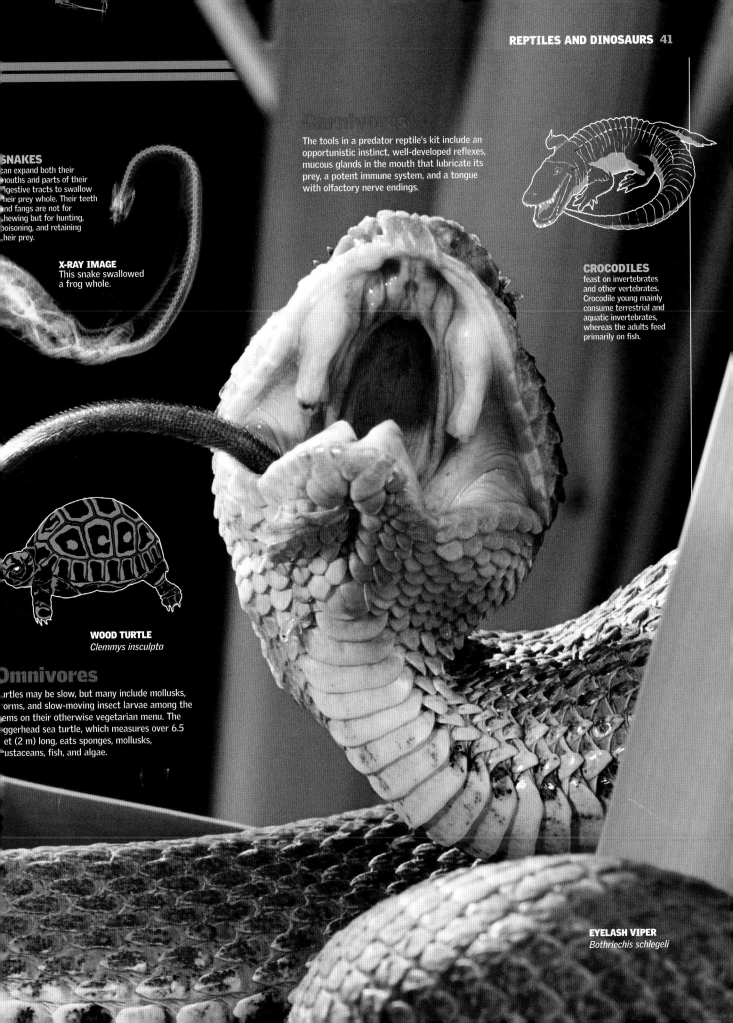

SNAKES

can expand both their
mouths and parts of their
digestive tracts to swallow
their prey whole. Their teeth
and fangs are not for
chewing but for hunting,
poisoning, and retaining
their prey.

X-RAY IMAGE
This snake swallowed
a frog whole.

Carnivores

The tools in a predator reptile's kit include an
opportunistic instinct, well-developed reflexes,
mucous glands in the mouth that lubricate its
prey, a potent immune system, and a tongue
with olfactory nerve endings.

CROCODILES
feast on invertebrates
and other vertebrates.
Crocodile young mainly
consume terrestrial and
aquatic invertebrates,
whereas the adults feed
primarily on fish.

WOOD TURTLE
Clemmys insculpta

Omnivores

Turtles may be slow, but many include mollusks,
worms, and slow-moving insect larvae among the
items on their otherwise vegetarian menu. The
loggerhead sea turtle, which measures over 6.5
feet (2 m) long, eats sponges, mollusks,
crustaceans, fish, and algae.

EYELASH VIPER
Bothriechis schlegeli

Reproduction

Most reptiles are oviparous. Some species lay large numbers of eggs and then allow them to develop on their own, generally in well-protected nests or hidden under dirt or sand. Marine turtles, especially green turtles, travel to the coast to lay their eggs in the sand, where they are left at the mercy of all who pass by. The females of other species, however, fiercely protect their offspring, staying near their nests for long periods of time to scare away potential predators. ●

GREEN ANACOND
Eunectes murinus
An anaconda can have more than 50 offspring which measure near 3 feet (1 m) long at birth.

Eggshells

Reptile offspring develop within a liquid-filled sac called the amnion, which lies inside the egg. Most reptile eggs have soft, flexible shells, but some have much harder shells. Through the shell, the hatchling absorbs the oxygen and moisture it needs for growth, while its yolk provides it with food.

Oviparous

Reproduction that involves laying eggs in which the offspring complete their development before hatching. Some species lay large numbers of eggs and then allow them to develop on their own, generally in well-protected nests or hidden in dirt or sand. In other species, such as crocodiles, the females fiercely protect their offspring.

THE FEMALE REPRODUCTIVE SYSTEM
has two ovaries that contain the ovules, leading into two oviducts that reach the cloaca. Fertilization occurs in the forward part of the oviduct.

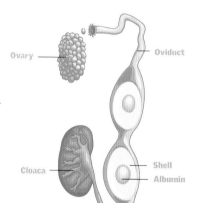

Ovary
Oviduct
Cloaca
Shell
Albumin
Cloaca

① Growth
The egg is buried by the mother, and the embryo begins to develop. The egg provides the necessary oxygen and food.

② Fracture
The pressure exerted on the shell from the movements of the animal within such a cramped space causes the shell to break from the inside.

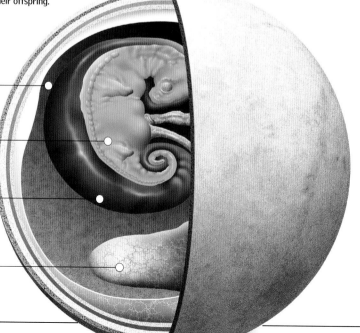

LEOPARD TORTOISE

SHELL
allows oxygen to enter, so the embryo can breathe.

EMBRYO
Protected from drying out, it can survive without water.

YOLK SAC
surrounds the embryo and stores food for its birth.

ALLANTOIS
Prolongation of the embryonic intestines

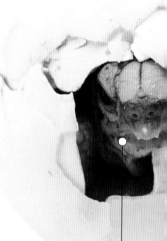

EGG TOOTH
A corneous, or horny, spine on the beak for breaking the shell during hatching

Ovoviviparous

The eggs remain in the mother's body, and hatching occurs there. The hatched young are diminutive versions of adult animals. Already independent, they do not receive any care from their parents.

145 to 160 days

IS THE INCUBATION PERIOD OF THE LEOPARD TORTOISE.

4

Exit

It can take the baby animal an entire day to exit, and it will have a small sac hanging from its navel. This is the sac of yolk that provided it with food while it was incubating.

MOUTH
is the first part to appear.

FOOT
already has mobility, thus allowing the baby reptile to walk.

CARAPACE (SHELL)
is already completely formed at birth.

3

Hatching

The turtle is ready to come out and starts to break the egg with its body. Hatching occurs.

CARAPACE
Its growth makes the egg break.

LEOPARD TORTOISE
Geochelone pardalis

Habitat	Africa
Diet	Herbivorous
Size	23-26 inches (60-65 cm)
Weight	77 pounds (35 kg)

FER-DE-LANCE
Bothrops atrox
In one litter, it can produce up to 80 offspring, each with a length of 13 inches (34 cm).

CONSISTENCY OF THE EGGS
The eggshell can be soft or hard. Soft eggshells are usually found in lizards and snakes, whereas hard eggshells are common in turtles and crocodiles.

Viviparous

As is the case with most mammals, the whole embryonic developmental cycle occurs inside the mother's body, and the embryo obtains food from close contact with maternal tissues.

Hard   **Soft**

Lizards and Crocodiles

Because of their long, powerful bodies and sharp teeth, crocodiles are among the most dangerous predators. When they are small, they eat small fish, frogs, and insects. When fully grown, however, they can devour large animals and even humans. We invite you to learn more about the life and habits of these animals. Did you know

hat lizards are the most numerous
eptiles in the world today? This
roup includes a wide variety of
pecies of all shapes and sizes. They
ll belong to the taxonomic group
Sauria, and most are carnivores. The
Komodo dragon of Indonesia eats wild
hogs, deer, and monkeys and can weigh
nearly 300 pounds (135 kg). ●

Lizards

Lizards are the largest group of reptiles. They live in most environments except for extremely cold regions, since they cannot regulate their own body temperatures. There are land-dwelling, underground, tree-dwelling, and even semi-aquatic lizards. They can walk, climb, dig, run, and even glide. Lizards often have differentiated heads, movable eyelids, a rigid lower jaw, four five-toed feet, a long body covered with scales, and a long tail. Some can even shed their tails when threatened. ●

DAY GECKOS
Phelsuma sp.

STICKY TOES

Chameleons

live in Africa, especially in southeastern regions and on Madagascar. They live in forests, where they use their prehensile tails and toes to climb trees. Their well-known ability to change color is important when they face danger or when they begin to court.

Camouflage

is an adaptive advantage. By blending in with the vegetation surrounding them, lizards can escape the notice of both their predators and their prey.

LIFESAVING RECOURSE
Between each vertebra, there are rupture planes enabling the tail to separate from the body.

AUTOTOMIC TAIL

Certain lizards can shed their tails many times during their lives. In dangerous situations, they may even shed it voluntarily in order to flee their confused predators. Later the tail grows back.

TELESCOPIC EYES

Geckos and Skinks

are lizard-like animals of the family Gekkonidae that live in warm regions. Their limbs are very small. (In fact, some species have none at all!) Their bodies are covered with smooth, shiny scales.

MELLER'S CHAMELEON
Chamaeleo melleri

SKIN
has cells with many pigments.

TAIL
curls up when necessary.

PREHENSILE TOES
can surround a branch and hold on tight.

CLAW

4,765

LIZARD SPECIES EXIST IN THE WORLD.

Heloderma

comprise only two species, which live in the United States and Mexico. They feed on invertebrates and small vertebrates. Their bodies are massive, and their skin is covered with small knobs. They are the only poisonous lizards, and their bite can be dangerous to humans.

COLORS
warn of poison.

GILA MONSTER
Heloderma suspectum

FAT TAIL
stores fat reserves for later consumption.

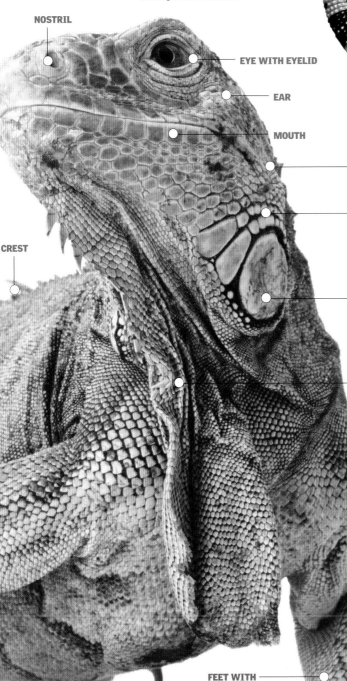

NOSTRIL

EYE WITH EYELID

EAR

MOUTH

CREST
runs from head to tail.

SKIN
has scales covered with a tough, corneous (or hornlike) layer.

SUBTYMPANIC SHIELD

CREST

DEWLAP
is fleshy and large in males.

COMMON IGUANA
Iguana sp.

FEET WITH CLAWS
enable it to walk, climb, and dig burrows.

Body Heat

Lizards survive in environments where they can maintain their body temperature, such as forests or deserts.

**SUNBATHING
6:00 AM**
The lizard places its body in the sun's rays to take advantage of their heat.

**IN ACTION
10:00 AM**
It begins its daily activities and movements.

**HIDDEN
12:00 PM**
When the sun is at its highest, they hide from the excessive heat.

**CATCHING A FEW MORE RAYS
6:00 PM**
They return to the sunlight but elevate their bodies to take advantage of the heat radiating from the rocks.

Iguanas

Iguanas belong to the largest New World group of reptiles and have the most complex design. They inhabit tropical regions of the Americas, including the forests of Mexico. They can change color during mating season. The species of this group are vegetarians.

Komodo Dragon

his animal is the largest lizard in the world. It is related to monitor lizards and can grow up to 9.8 feet (3 m) long and weigh up to approximately 330 pounds (150 kg). These endangered lizards live only on a group of islands in Indonesia. They are carnivorous and are known for their ferocity in attacking their prey. Their saliva is full of bacteria that can kill their prey with only one bite. They can detect other Komodo dragons from several miles away.

INDONESIA

Banta

Sumbawa

KOMODO NATIONAL PARK

Padar

Nusa

Komodo

Rinca

Kode

Montong

KOMODO DRAGON
Varanus komodoensis

| Habitat (approx.) | 900 square miles (2,300 sq km) |
| Number of Dragons | Less than 5,000 |

TOUGH SKIN
is covered with black, brown, or dark gray scales.

CLAWS
Its five claws are very sharp. It uses them to hold onto its dying prey.

SIZE AND WEIGHT
Males can grow more than 10 feet long. Females are somewhat smaller.

Weight
330 pounds (150 kg)
9.8 feet (3 m)
Komodo Dragon

Weight
22 pounds (10 kg)
3.3 feet (1 m)
Iguana

6 feet (1.8 m)

Weight
175 pounds (80 kg)
Human

STOMACH
Like most reptiles, Komodo dragons have a stomach that can expand enormously. This enables them to gulp down up to 70 percent of their own weight in a single meal.

How It Attacks Its Prey

A Long Hunt

Komodo dragons have an acute sense of smell that can detect the presence of other animals up to 2 miles (3 km) away. They track their prey using their forked tongues to detect scents from molecules in the air. Jacobson's organ, located inside the mouth, helps the lizard to locate its prey more rapidly and consume less energy while tracking it.

1 SEARCH
The dragon searches for food with its forked tongue. When chasing its prey, it can reach speeds of up to 11 miles (18 km) per hour.

5,000

LIZARDS
of the family Varanidae live in the wild on six small Indonesian islands, including Komodo Island.

SMELL
They have an acute sense of smell that can detect the odor of decomposing flesh at a distance of up to 3 miles (5 km).

2 BITE
Following the scent, the dragon captures its prey, which dies after being bitten. Its favorite prey is deer and wild boars.

SALIVA
contains bacteria that are harmful to its prey. Antibacterial substances in the Komodo dragon's blood protect it from their harmful effects.

3 FEEDING
The dragon feeds rapidly, using the flexible joints of its jaws and skull. It digests not only chunks of meat but also the skin and bones of its prey.

TONGUE
is forked and is used for tasting, smelling, and feeling. It can perceive various airborne particles, helping it detect prey.

4 STRUGGLE
Smelling a meal, more dragons approach. The largest get the best portions. The younger ones keep their distance, since the adults may act as cannibals.

Deadly Saliva

The saliva of Komodo dragons is full of bacteria that can quickly kill its prey by causing septicemia. To kill its prey, the Komodo dragon only needs to bite it once. An analysis of its saliva revealed 60 types of bacteria, 54 of which cause infection. These bacteria are known to cause putrefaction of dead animals, including the bacteria *Pasteurella multocida* (one of the deadliest), *Streptococcus*, *Staphylococcus*, *Pseudomonas*, and *Klebsiella*. When combined, they are a deadly weapon.

PASTEURELLA MULTOCIDA
Bacteria that affects the gastrointestinal and respiratory tracts of mammals and birds

Marine Iguana

The Galapagos Islands, besides serving as a home for many species of the Central Pacific and South America, also have an amazing number of indigenous species. One of these is the marine iguana, the only species of iguana in the world that spends most of its time in the water. This reptile lives on the rocky coasts and feeds on seaweed and algae. It can stay underwater for 45 minutes and dive approximately 50 feet (15 m) deep. This unique, slow-swimming creature gathers seaweed to eat at low tide or dives for food. ●

Life in Colonies

The marine iguana is native to the Galapagos Islands and is the only lizard that finds its food in the sea. It lives in colonies, which is a curiosity given the solitary behavior of other iguanas. When they are not feeding, marine iguanas stretch out on rocks to warm in the sun. Thousands may be seen on one area of the beach. However, their peaceful coexistence disappears during mating season when males fight aggressively over females. The females reestablish harmony at nesting time. Since there is little space for the nests, thousands of females lay their eggs together. Each one can lay from one to six eggs, which are placed in a sandy burrow.

SCALY BACK

LEGS
are kept to the side of the body while swimming.

TAIL
can be used as a whip in self-defense.

MARINE IGUANA
Amblyrhynchus cristatus

Habit	Semi-aquatic
Length	20-40 inches (50-100 cm)
Range	Galapagos Islands

Weight
24 pounds
(11 kg)

40 inches (1 m)

Pinta

Roca Redonda

Marchena

Genovesa

Equator 0°

Santiago

Bartolomé

Seymour

Rábida   Baltra

Fernandina

Santa Cruz   San Cristóbal

Pinzón

Santa Fe

Isabela

GALAPAGOS ISLANDS

91°   90°

Floreana
(Isla Santa Maria)

Española

The Galapagos Islands

consist of 13 major islands, six small islands, and many islets, all of which are volcanic in origin. Located along the Equator, some 620 miles (1,000 km) west of the South American landmass, they are part of the territory of Ecuador. Their climate varies widely because of the different ocean currents that converge around the archipelago. Because of their isolation, they are home to many indigenous species, most of which are birds and reptiles.

45 MINUTES UNDERWATER WITHOUT AIR

is the maximum amount of time that a marine iguana can stay submerged while looking for food.

SPINES

The crest is usually larger in males. When fighting for a female, they strike their crests against their opponents.

Swimming

English naturalist Charles Darwin described the marine iguana's style of swimming as "agile and rapid," but later studies and observations revealed the opposite. This animal, found only on the Galapagos Islands, swims very slowly and with very little energy. The fastest swimming speed recorded for a marine iguana was 2.8 feet (0.85 m) per second, and it only maintained this pace for two minutes. The average speed for a marine iguana is a mere 1.5 feet (0.45 m) per second, and only the largest iguanas are strong enough to swim above the waves.

Its tail is thick and flat.

Wavelike movements of its body propel it forward.

Its legs are bent to the side.

Feeding Habits

The largest marine iguanas eat seaweed in the water, but the smaller and younger ones do not. Although adult iguanas can dive to a depth of about 50 feet (15 m), in normal conditions they feed at low tide in dives that last less than 10 minutes. Young iguanas, however, stay out of the water because their body temperature could fall rapidly. They can only feed on seaweed that grows on exposed rocks and is deposited at high tide.

SALT

Between its eyes and its nostrils, the marine iguana has glands to expel salt from its body. By exhaling strongly, it emits a jet of air that scatters the salt, which falls on its head and forms a white crest.

SEAWEED

The different kinds of seaweed that grow on the islands may cause these reptiles to vary in color from one island to another.

Out of the wather
They sun themselves on the coast, where their colonies live.

CLAWS

are longer and sharper than those of land-dwelling iguanas, allowing the animals to cling to rocks to avoid being swept away by waves.

HIGH TIDE
12 hours

Sea Level

Intermediate Zone
They walk or dive for food, depending on the tide level.

Seaweed

LOW TIDE
12 hours

Diving Zone
Seaweed is abundant but can only be reached by diving.

Geckos

Geckos are a group of small, slender lizard species that live mostly in tropical and subtropical regions and on many islands in the oceans. Some species live in deserts, and many have burrows or make their homes in rock crevices. They are nocturnal and can flee from their predators by voluntarily shedding their tails. Geckos are the only lizards whose males produce sounds to attract females and to defend their territory. These agile climbers can walk on smooth vertical surfaces or even upside down by using tiny hairs on their feet that let them stick to anything they touch.

Leaf-Tailed Gecko

When hanging by its tail, it looks exactly like a leaf, which gave rise to its common name. Male geckos can produce sounds similar to vocalized calls. In this species, they are especially loud and high-pitched.

—————— 10 inches (25 cm) ——————

LEAF-TAILED GECKO

Scientific name	*Uroplatus henkeli*
Family	Gekkonidae
Habitat	Trees
Range	Madagascar, Africa
Diet	Carnivorous (insects)

Flight of the Gecko

The Kuhl's flying gecko lives in trees in Southeast Asia. Unlike flying lizards, it glides with its webbed feet. When it is not "flying," it spends most of its time hanging head down in the trees, ready for a rapid takeoff.

1,050
SPECIES ARE IN THE GECKO FAMILY

Its tail is autotomic, meaning that the gecko can shed it, allowing the reptile to double its speed.

Its muscular legs are those of a great climber.

 Spreading Its Limbs
The membranes between its toes are used as wings for gliding.

 Arching Its Back
The membranes along its sides and flat tail help it to regulate its fall.

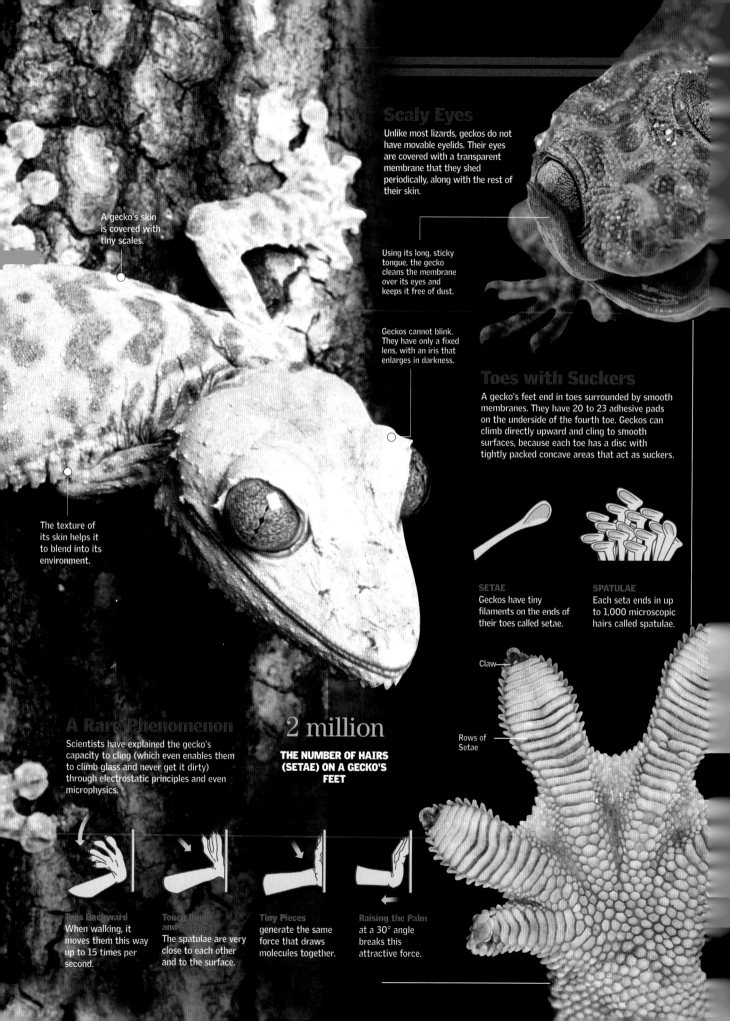

Scaly Eyes

Unlike most lizards, geckos do not have movable eyelids. Their eyes are covered with a transparent membrane that they shed periodically, along with the rest of their skin.

Using its long, sticky tongue, the gecko cleans the membrane over its eyes and keeps it free of dust.

Geckos cannot blink. They have only a fixed lens, with an iris that enlarges in darkness.

A gecko's skin is covered with tiny scales.

The texture of its skin helps it to blend into its environment.

Toes with Suckers

A gecko's feet end in toes surrounded by smooth membranes. They have 20 to 23 adhesive pads on the underside of the fourth toe. Geckos can climb directly upward and cling to smooth surfaces, because each toe has a disc with tightly packed concave areas that act as suckers.

SETAE
Geckos have tiny filaments on the ends of their toes called setae.

SPATULAE
Each seta ends in up to 1,000 microscopic hairs called spatulae.

Claw

Rows of Setae

A Rare Phenomenon

Scientists have explained the gecko's capacity to cling (which even enables them to climb glass and never get it dirty) through electrostatic principles and even microphysics.

2 million

THE NUMBER OF HAIRS (SETAE) ON A GECKO'S FEET

Toes Backward
When walking, it moves them this way up to 15 times per second.

Touch Down and Cling
The spatulae are very close to each other and to the surface.

Tiny Pieces
generate the same force that draws molecules together.

Raising the Palm
at a 30° angle breaks this attractive force.

Changing Colors

Chameleons are well known for their ability to change color. Another interesting fact is that their tongue can stretch great distances in seconds. They live mostly in Africa. Their prehensile tails and toes make them excellent climbers. Another helpful characteristic is that their eyes can move independently of one another, providing them a 360° field of vision. Their flat bodies help them to balance and to hide among the leaves.

PREHENSILE TAIL
They use their long curved tails to hold on to branches without using their feet.

BONE
acts as a support for discharging the tongue.

Protractible Tongue

Long and lightweight, the chameleon's tongue is sticky and can be extended. Chameleons throw their tongues outward like projectiles to hunt their prey.

1 Contraction

Several sheets of collagen between the tongue and the accelerating muscle are compressed in the form of a spiral, which stores the energy necessary to propel the tongue outward.

Up to 600%
of the tongue's length is curled up in reserve.

How It Changes Color

The color-changing ability of chameleons, well known in popular sayings and songs, is not an adaptation to the environment as is widely believed. Rather it is related to changes in light and temperature, courtship behaviors, or the presence of a predator. Color changes are caused by the action of hormones on pigment cells in the skin. These specialized cells, located in each layer of the dermis, react and change color, camouflaging the chameleon from its predators.

A When the upper layer (chromatophores) detects a yellow color, the blue light of the guanophores (white chromatophores) becomes greenish.

PIGMENT CELLS

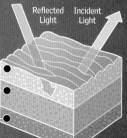

Reflected Light   Incident Light

Chromatophores

Guanophores

Melanophores

PANTHER CHAMELEON
Furcifer pardalis

Range	Madagascar
Habitat	Coastal Regions
Lifestyle	Diurnal

14-20 inches (35-50 cm)

Feeding Habits

These diurnal hunters wait for victims to pass by. Their diet includes arthropods and small invertebrates. Among insects, they prefer crickets, grubs, cockroaches, and moths. Other species on the menu also include songbirds and mice.

TIP
The tip of the tongue spreads out and captures the prey with its sticky surface.

TONGUE
Covered with collagen tissue.

2 Unfolding
The accelerating muscle compresses the energy-storing collagen tissues, launching the tongue toward its target.

3 Retraction
When the elastic tissues contract again, they roll up the tongue and return it to its initial position with the prey sticking to it.

FEET
The toes are divided into two parts, with two toes on the outside and three on the inside.

2 Toes

3 Toes

B The melanophores contain a dark pigment called melanin, which regulates the brightness and the amount of light reflected, varying its color.

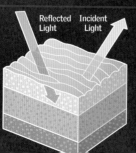

Reflected Light   Incident Light

Venerated and Feared

Crocodiles—along with their relatives, the alligators, caimans, and gavials—are very ancient animals. They belong to the same group that included the dinosaurs and have changed very little in the last 65 million years. They can go for long periods without moving; during these times, they sun themselves or rest in the water. However, they can also swim, jump, and even run at high speed to attack with force and precision. In spite of their ferocity, female crocodiles provide more care for their young than any other living group of reptiles. ●

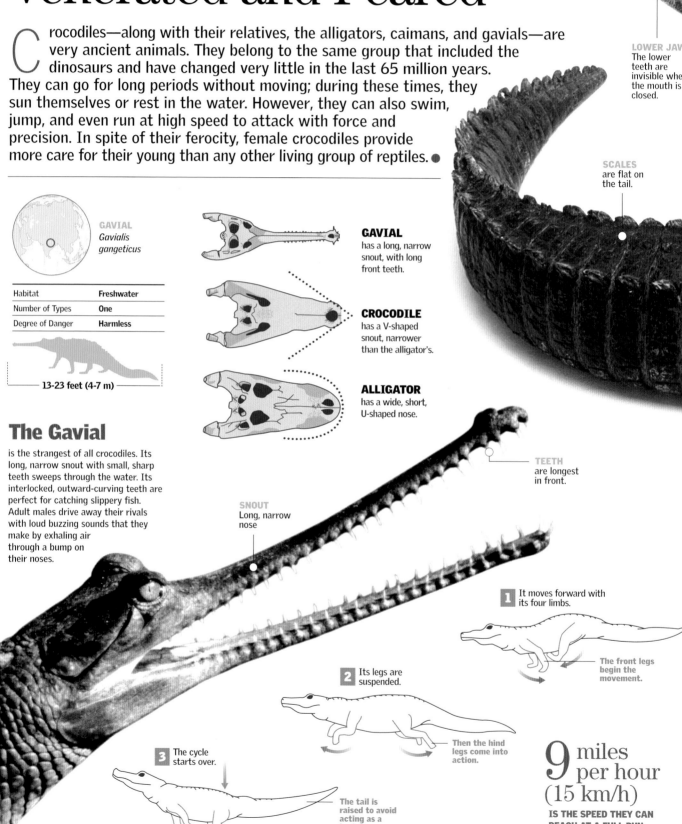

LOWER JAW
The lower teeth are invisible when the mouth is closed.

SCALES
are flat on the tail.

GAVIAL
Gavialis gangeticus

Habitat	Freshwater
Number of Types	One
Degree of Danger	Harmless

13-23 feet (4-7 m)

GAVIAL
has a long, narrow snout, with long front teeth.

CROCODILE
has a V-shaped snout, narrower than the alligator's.

ALLIGATOR
has a wide, short, U-shaped nose.

The Gavial

is the strangest of all crocodiles. Its long, narrow snout with small, sharp teeth sweeps through the water. Its interlocked, outward-curving teeth are perfect for catching slippery fish. Adult males drive away their rivals with loud buzzing sounds that they make by exhaling air through a bump on their noses.

SNOUT
Long, narrow nose

TEETH
are longest in front.

1 It moves forward with its four limbs.

The front legs begin the movement.

2 Its legs are suspended.

Then the hind legs come into action.

3 The cycle starts over.

The tail is raised to avoid acting as a brake.

9 miles per hour (15 km/h)

IS THE SPEED THEY CAN REACH AT A FULL RUN.

CLAWS

Habitat	**Freshwater**
Number of Types	**Eight**
Diet	**Insects, Mammals, Birds**

10 to 20 feet (3-6 m)

SCALES

Alligators and Caimans

Alligators and caimans are almost completely limited to freshwater. They make their nests by piling up grass, dirt, and leaves to lay their hard-shelled eggs. The female often remains near the nest to keep would-be thieves from invading. Although they look clumsy, alligators can use their jaws with precision. The female often helps her eggs to hatch by putting them in her mouth, where she rolls them against her palate with her tongue until they crack.

JOINT

NILE
CROCODILE
*Crocodylos
niloticus*

Habitat	**Freshwater and Saltwater**
Number of Types	**One**
Life Span	**70 years**

16 to 20 feet (5-6 m)

How They Move

Although their preferred form of movement is swimming or crawling, crocodiles can run for short distances if they feel threatened. They can reach speeds of up to 9 miles per hour (15 km/h) when running, with their abdomens supported above their knees and their elbows slightly bent. They can go even faster when sliding on mud.

TEETH
number from 64 to 68. The fourth tooth on the lower jaw is visible when the mouth is closed.

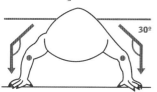

30°

POSTURE
Semi-crouched. The knees and elbows are slightly bent.

SWIMMING
Using its tail for locomotion, it moves with agility through the water.

Crocodiles

have four feet. In this way, they are very similar to lizards. They are distinguished by their great size and ferocity. Several rows of bony plates that look like spines or teeth run down the length of their back. They can stay in the water for long periods of time, and they are able to swallow underwater without drowning. They make their nests in holes on the beach. The Johnston's, or freshwater, crocodile, of tropical northern Australia, can gallop to the water by raising all four feet off the ground.

The Largest on the Nile

he impressive Nile crocodile is considered one of the most dangerous animals in Africa. It is one of three crocodile species that live in Africa and one of the largest species in the world. It can reach nearly 20 feet (6 m) in length and weigh over 2,200 pounds (1,000 kg). It lives in freshwater lakes and rivers. This dark olive-colored giant has a terrible reputation for devouring humans. For this reason, it has been both hated and revered, especially in ancient Egypt, where crocodiles were mummified and worshipped.

Range

Nile crocodiles live all along the Nile River and throughout sub-Saharan Africa. They are also found in ocean waters near the African continent and the island of Madagascar. They inhabit river deltas, lakes, large swamps, and estuaries and are currently raised in many countries, such as Kenya, Tanzania, Israel, Indonesia, France, Japan, and Spain.

NILE CROCODILE
Cocodrylus niloticus

Class	Reptilia
Length	20 feet (6 m)
Range	Africa
Weight	2,200 pounds (1,000 kg)

Weight 2,200 pounds (1,000 kg)
20 feet (6 m)

6 feet (1.8 m)

Weight 175 pounds (80 kg)

Habits

On land, crocodiles usually crawl on their bellies, although they can also raise their bodies and walk or run with their legs extended. Since they constantly need an external heat source, it is common to see them sunning themselves with their jaws open. This allows the breeze to cool the membranes of their mouths, regulating their body temperature. They are perfectly adapted for life in the water and use their tails for swimming.

SCALES ALONG THE BACK

WELL PROTECTED
Body scales serve as armor. Webbed feet help them to swim.

EYES ON TOP OF HEAD

V-SHAPED SNOUT

Implacable Hunter

▶ The Nile crocodile is a phenomenal predator. It can eat fish, antelope, zebras, and even buffalo. It can also jump out of the water to capture birds from their nests. In spite of their solitary habits, several crocodiles may join together to eat and work as a team to corral fish in shallow waters. They eat animals that approach the water's edge to drink by dragging them into the water to drown them and then tearing them to pieces.

1 Stalk
Using a stealth surprising because of its large size, the Nile crocodile stalks its prey until trapping it.

WARTHOG
Phacochoerus africanus

Eyes out of the water

2 Attack
When hunting large prey, it attacks when they approach the water to drink.

3 Drown
Once it has the prey clenched in its jaws, it pulls it into the water and keeps it submerged until it drowns.

1 hour
THE AMOUNT OF TIME THEY CAN REMAIN UNDERWATER

Busy Females

▶ The female lays from 16 to 80 eggs in a hole well above the water level. She will use this same nest throughout her life. She carefully protects the eggs while they incubate. When the young hatch, she carefully picks up the hatchlings and carries them to the water in groups. Mother and offspring stay together for six to eight weeks and then gradually separate.

HATCHLING
The young crocodiles will live in burrows up to 10 feet (3 m) long for the first four years of their lives.

The American Example

aimans also belong to the order of crocodilians. These fierce reptiles live exclusively in the tropical regions of the Americas, mainly in lakes and swampy regions. Occasionally, when looking for food, they enter areas populated by humans. The caiman family includes the genera *Caiman*, *Melanosuchus*, and *Paleosuchus*. The largest species is the black caiman, so named because of the color of its hide.

Black Predator

The black caiman is distinguished from other caimans by dark stripes on the lower part of its mouth and yellow lines along the sides of its body. However, it is similar to other caimans in its feeding habits, which depend on its age. Young caimans feed on arthropods and amphibians, while adults eat fish, birds, and mammals, or snails if other foods are scarce. Caimans do not have a large appetite. For example, in captivity they consume only 14 ounces (400 g) of meat twice a week.

BLACK CAIMAN
Melanosuchus niger

Habitat	Equatorial Amazon River
Lifestyle	Aquatic
Length	8-10 feet (2.4-3 m)
Life Span	30 years

Weight
880 pounds
(400 kg)

15 feet (4.5 m)

6 feet
(1.8 m)

Weight
175 pounds
(80 kg)

99%

DROP IN NUMBERS
This species is in danger of extinction because of poaching.

Reproduction

Caimans mate in the water. Once the eggs have been fertilized, the females begin to build their nest, forming a mound out of dry vegetation and earth. With their hind legs, they dig a hole in the center where they lay their eggs—from 30 to 75 at a time. When finished, they cover the nest with earth. In some cases, the females return to the water and have nothing more to do with the eggs.

NEST
The eggs that are exposed to the air, which are not kept as warm, will hatch as females.

FUTURE FEMALES

FUTURE MALES

MOTHER WITH YOUNG
Some females fiercely defend their offspring.

BRANCHES AND DRY LEAVES

Melanosuchus niger
BLACK CAIMAN

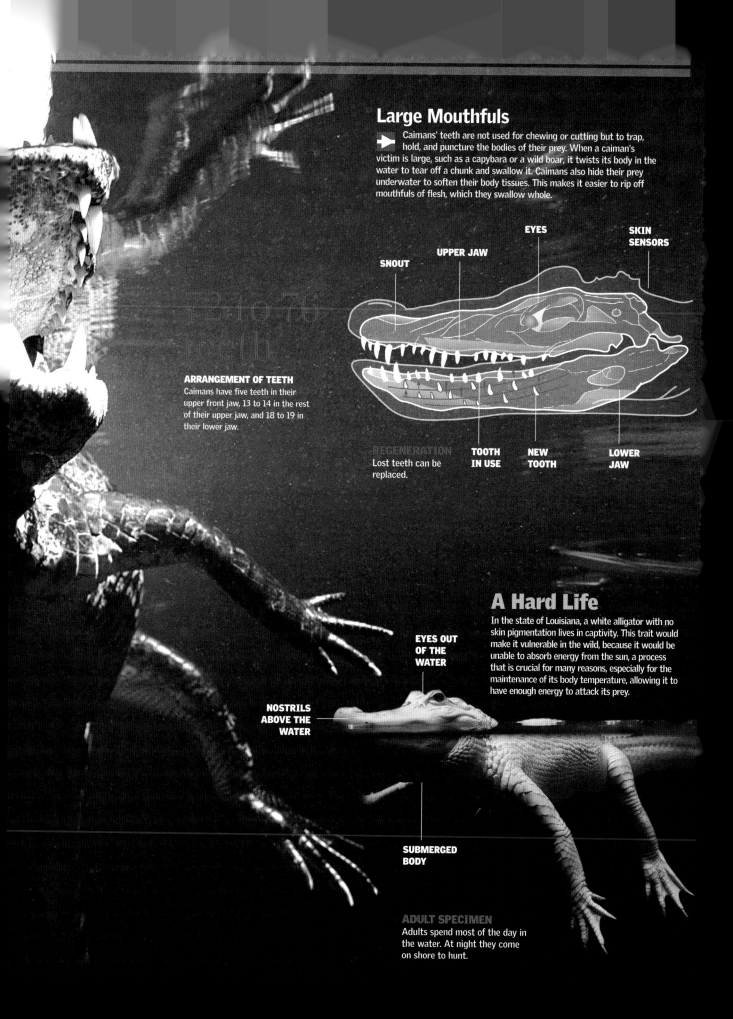

Large Mouthfuls

➡ Caimans' teeth are not used for chewing or cutting but to trap, hold, and puncture the bodies of their prey. When a caiman's victim is large, such as a capybara or a wild boar, it twists its body in the water to tear off a chunk and swallow it. Caimans also hide their prey underwater to soften their body tissues. This makes it easier to rip off mouthfuls of flesh, which they swallow whole.

ARRANGEMENT OF TEETH
Caimans have five teeth in their upper front jaw, 13 to 14 in the rest of their upper jaw, and 18 to 19 in their lower jaw.

SNOUT

UPPER JAW

EYES

SKIN SENSORS

REGENERATION
Lost teeth can be replaced.

TOOTH IN USE

NEW TOOTH

LOWER JAW

A Hard Life

In the state of Louisiana, a white alligator with no skin pigmentation lives in captivity. This trait would make it vulnerable in the wild, because it would be unable to absorb energy from the sun, a process that is crucial for many reasons, especially for the maintenance of its body temperature, allowing it to have enough energy to attack its prey.

EYES OUT OF THE WATER

NOSTRILS ABOVE THE WATER

SUBMERGED BODY

ADULT SPECIMEN
Adults spend most of the day in the water. At night they come on shore to hunt.

Turtles and Snakes

I n this chapter, you will discover the amazing world of turtles and snakes. You will learn what they are like inside, where they live, and how they hunt their prey, as well as why some eat only eggs and others, such as constrictors (the most primitive snakes), have to suffocate their prey by coiling around it. This chapter will also reveal interesting

GREEN TREE PYTHON
This tree-dwelling green python usually coils around a branch and waits with its head hanging down, ready to attack. It eats small mammals and birds.

...acts about turtles' skeletons and ...hells (for example, turtles that swim ...ave streamlined shells that enable ...hem to glide easily through the water). ...lthough people may think that turtles are peaceful creatures, many are actually carnivorous hunters that eat small invertebrates, fish, and even some larger animals.●

Slow but Steady

Since their appearance on Earth about 230 million years ago, turtles have changed very little. Turtles can live on land, in freshwater, or in saltwater. However, they all need light and heat to survive, and they all lay their eggs on land. Although aquatic turtles are nearly all carnivorous, some land-dwelling species are herbivorous. Turtles' most noticeable trait is their hard shell, which encloses and protects the soft part of their bodies. It also camouflages them for protection from predator species. ●

HEAD
has a pointed nose.

NECK
Much longer than that of other species

Freshwater Turtles

Most turtle species live in freshwater. They are distinguished by their feet, which are partially or totally webbed and are used for swimming, an activity at which they are highly skilled. They can also be identified by their shells, which are flatter than those of land-dwelling turtles. Some freshwater turtles are quite well adapted to living on land. In general, they prefer warm climates with abundant vegetation, so they commonly live near swamps and rivers located in subtropical areas around the world. Their shells may have particular characteristics depending on the species. The American box turtle, for example, can completely close its shell..

APPROXIMATELY

300-350
TURTLE SPECIES EXIST.

SHELL
This species has a very soft, thin shell.

TYPES OF SHELLS
Turtle shells differ according to each species' habitat.

STREAMLINED
Leatherback Turtle

FLAT
Red-Eared Slider

CRESTED
Alligator Snapping Turtle

Chinese Soft-Shelled Turtle
Pelodiscus sinensis
They live in swamps and streams. Their diet consists of fish and mollusks.

Ocean Species

...re the rarest. They live in warm waters and are excellent swimmers.
...hey have flippers instead of feet. The front flippers move them
...orward, and the back flippers act as a rudder for steering. Their shells
...f oceanic turtles are flattened into a streamlined shape. These turtles
...ave developed a dual respiratory system that allows them to remain
...ubmerged for up to two hours.

SHELL
Small, flat, and joined
to the skeleton

...awksbill Turtle
...retmochelys imbricata
...ea turtles are usually heavy and
...arge. This Caribbean species can
...eigh up to 141 pounds (64 kg).

Concealed from Danger

Many scientists believe that turtles' shells
enabled them to survive long ago, during a
...me when so many other reptile species,
...cluding dinosaurs, perished. The shell consists of
... domed back and a flat belly, joined by a bridge
...etween the front and hind legs. The outer layer
... made of skin and hornlike plates, and the inner
...yer is made of bone. Turtles draw their heads
...side their shells in different ways depending on
...hether their necks are straight or side-bending.
...and-dwelling turtles have shells that enable
...em to hide their legs, as well as their heads,
...side, protecting their entire bodies from threats.
...he skeletons of ocean turtles, however, are
...ompletely integrated with their shells.

SIDE-NECKED TURTLE

Head
The neck bends to one side.

Legs and Tail
are always outside the shell.

STRAIGHT-NECKED TURTLE

Head
is pulled inside the shell by a vertical pendulum mechanism.

Legs and Tail
fold upward and are brought inside.

A Turtle's Age
Counting the successive hornlike plates that grow on the shell each year allows us to determine a turtle's age.

...SHELL
...Made of shieldlike
...plates

PLASTRON
Underside of the shell

Hermann's Tortoise
Testudo hermanni

On Solid Ground

Land-dwelling species have the best-protected legs because they are covered by large scales. They also have the most dome-shaped shells. Many species have front legs that are adapted for digging deep burrows, which serve as a shelter in inclement weather and protect them from threats from other species. The Florida gopher tortoise (*Gopherus polyphemus*) can dig tunnels up to 33 feet (10 m) deep. Some land-dwelling species can inflict very painful scratches.

Long-Lived Giants

Giant tortoises once lived on all the continents except Australia and Antarctica, both before and during the Pleistocene Era. They are now extinct on the continents and are only found on the Aldabra atoll in the Seychelles islands in the Indian Ocean and on the Galapagos Islands off the coast of Ecuador. In the Galapagos there are distinct populations living in different parts of its small area. The Galapagos giant tortoise, *Geochelone nigra*, is the largest tortoise in the world, weighing up to 880 pounds (400 kg). The oldest one still living is over 175 years old.

GALAPAGOS GIANT TORTOISE
Geochelone elephantopus

Habitat	Galapagos Islands
Diet	Herbivorous
Height	Up to 47 inches (120 cm)
Length	Up to 59 inches (150 cm)

Roca Redonda

Pinta
(home of
"Lonesome
George")

Genovesa

Marchena

Equator 0°

Santiago

Bartolomé

Seymour

Baltra

Rábida

San Cristóbal

Fernandina

Santa Cruz

Pinzón

Santa Fe

GALAPAGOS ISLANDS

Isabela

Floreana

Española

LONESOME GEORGE
is the nickname of the
only survivor of a now
extinct subspecies
(*G. nigra abindoni*).

1
Reproduction

Mating
is rather aggressive; the
male immobilizes the
female in order to mount
and fertilize her.

The Life Cycle
Up to four months can pass between the time a
new turtle is conceived and the time it hatches.
Laying eggs takes several hours of work, and a
female can lose up to 20 percent of her weight
during this process. The large size of Galapagos
tortoises makes them lazy; they spend most of
their time sunning themselves in small groups on
warm, dry volcanic soils near the coast or a
swamp. Some eat carrion.

5
10 Years

Most Stable
Size
After this point, its rate
of growth slows.

2

Egg Laying
During the reproductive season,
the female lays eggs every two
weeks and makes from three to
eight nests.

3
Two Months Later

Hatching
After hatching, the young
climb to the surface,
usually at night.

4
Some Years

Development
The animal reaches
reproductive age, and
it will keep growing
throughout its life.

2.5 inches (6 cm)

Giant Egg
Its shell is hard
and spherical.

Almost 1,000 eggs

CAN BE LAID BY A FEMALE IN ONE SEASON. HOWEVER, VERY FEW YOUNG TORTOISES SURVIVE.

HUMPED BACK
enables it to stretch its neck upward.

RETRACTABLE NECK
enables it to hide its head inside its shell.

LONG NECK
can reach the leaves of bushes.

SHELL
weighs over 550 pounds (250 kg), enough to crush a human.

FRONT LEGS
are useful for climbing.

SCALES
are typical of this order of reptiles.

CLAWS
are used for digging.

Nesting

For nearly five hours, the female digs a funnel-shaped hole with her claws, softening the ground with her urine. She settles the eggs in layers, covers them with earth, and smoothes it down.

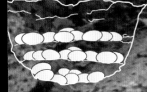

Giants

There are now 11 subspecies of Galapagos tortoises, including water-dwelling and land-dwelling varieties. All are in danger of extinction. They differ in maximum sizes, shell shapes, and neck lengths.

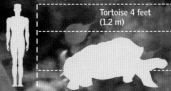

Human 6 feet (1.8 m)
Tortoise 4 feet (1.2 m)
Chaco Tortoise 0.8 foot (0.25 m)

CLOSE RELATIVES
The Chaco tortoise (*Geochelone chilensis*) is a continental ancestor.

Almost 14 months

THE LENGTH OF TIME A TORTOISE CAN LIVE WITHOUT EATING OR DRINKING

PLATES
are pointed, in the case of Asian tortoises.

BRIDGE
joins the upper shell to the plastron.

Main Predators

In addition to suffering from poaching humans in the past, Galapagos tortoises are in danger of extinction because of the low survival rate of their hatchlings, which are hunted by two types of species that have been introduced to their habitat: black rats and cats. Furthermore, the diet of adult female tortoises causes them to compete for food with goats and other livestock, more species not native to the tortoises' ecosystem.

ANIMALS INTRODUCED BY HUMANS

RATS

GOATS

DOGS

HOGS

Turtles in the Water!

S ea turtles have had to adapt parts of their bodies to an aquatic environment. Their front legs propel them through the water, and their hind legs serve as rudders for steering. Their shells are highly streamlined. They can spend up to several hours submerged in the water, since they have a dual respiratory system. They lay eggs but make their nests on solid ground, and they have an interesting system for choosing the spot where their young will be born—they return to the same spot where they, themselves, were born.

GREEN SEA TURTLE
Chelonia mydas

Habitat	Tropical and Subtropical Waters
Diet	Herbivorous
Length	Up to 39 inches (100 cm)
Life Span	50 years (estimated)

Habitat

When winter arrives, sea turtles migrate in warm ocean currents, such as the Gulf Stream, to places with higher temperatures. However, they sometimes stay too long in these currents, which then vanish, leaving the turtles in frigid water.

DEPTHS
Using their flippers to make powerful strokes, sea turtles move through the water in a manner resembling flying.

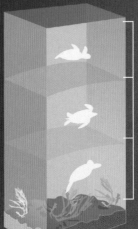

100 feet (30 m)
Kemp's Ridley Turtle

230 feet (70 m)
Green Sea Turtle

3,300 feet (1,000 m)
Leatherback Turtle

1,500 pounds (680 kg)

The leatherback turtle can measure up to 9 feet (2.7 m) long and weigh up to 1,500 pounds (680 kg).

HEAD
is relatively large and cannot be retracted into the shell.

EYE
has a double pair of eyelids.

LEATHERBACK TURTLE
Dermochelys coriacea

MODIFIED FEET
have become relatively large flippers.

FLIPPERS
Extension of the bones that make up the main part of the limb

BONY PLATES
are embedded in a thick, leathery, smooth skin, which gives the turtle the name leatherback. Its oily skin helps it to maintain its internal body temperature.

CLAW
Digit adapted for swimming

Sizes

Sea turtles' measurements vary widely by species. The largest living species is the leatherback, and the smallest is Kemp's ridley.

Kemp's Ridley
2 feet (65 cm)

Hawksbill
3 feet (90 cm)

Loggerhead
4 feet (110 cm)

Green
5 feet (140 cm)

Leatherback
6 feet (180 cm)

GREEN SEA TURTLE SHELL

LEATHERBACK TURTLE SHELL

PRECENTRAL SHIELD

FOUR LATERAL SHIELDS

KEELS

Reproduction

The reproductive cycle of sea turtles repeats every year, every two years, or every three years. Nesting is done during the summer on sandy beaches in tropical and subtropical areas where the average water temperature at the surface is always above 75° F (24° C). Every one, two, or three years, the turtles return from their feeding areas, which can be several hundred or even several thousand miles from their nesting sites. Apparently the turtles are able to memorize the exact location where they were born. They seem to navigate by ocean currents and temperatures.

MIGRATION TO BREEDING AREAS

MATING

MIGRATION FROM BIRTH AREA

EGG LAYING

HATCHLINGS

SHELL
is aerodynamical in shape—convex on the upper side and nearly flat on the underside.

PLASTRON
consists of lateral shields that are gray or greenish-gray.

Breathing
Sea turtles have wedge-shaped lungs that lie underneath their shells and are attached to their backs along the spine. Sea turtles can also breathe through their skin.

22 miles per hour (35 km/h)

THE SWIMMING SPEED OF
SEA TURTLES

Swimming

To be able to swim, turtles needed to adapt their front limbs and transform them into large flippers. Their hind limbs took the form of oars. They have a membrane around the bones of their phalanges (where their digits would be) and a shell that lies flat along their backs, giving them a streamlined shape.

The turtle rises and falls in the water according to the rhythm of its flippers.

FLYING
The flippers give a powerful stroke that resembles flight as the turtles move through the water.

The hind flippers are used as oars, pushing the turtle forward.

Internal Structure

Snakes are scaly reptiles with long bodies and no legs. Some are poisonous, but others are not. Like all reptiles, they have a spinal column and a skeletal structure composed of a system of vertebrae. The anatomical differences between species reveal information about their habitats and diets—climbing snakes are long and thin, burrowing snakes are shorter and thicker, and sea snakes have flat tails that they use as fins. ●

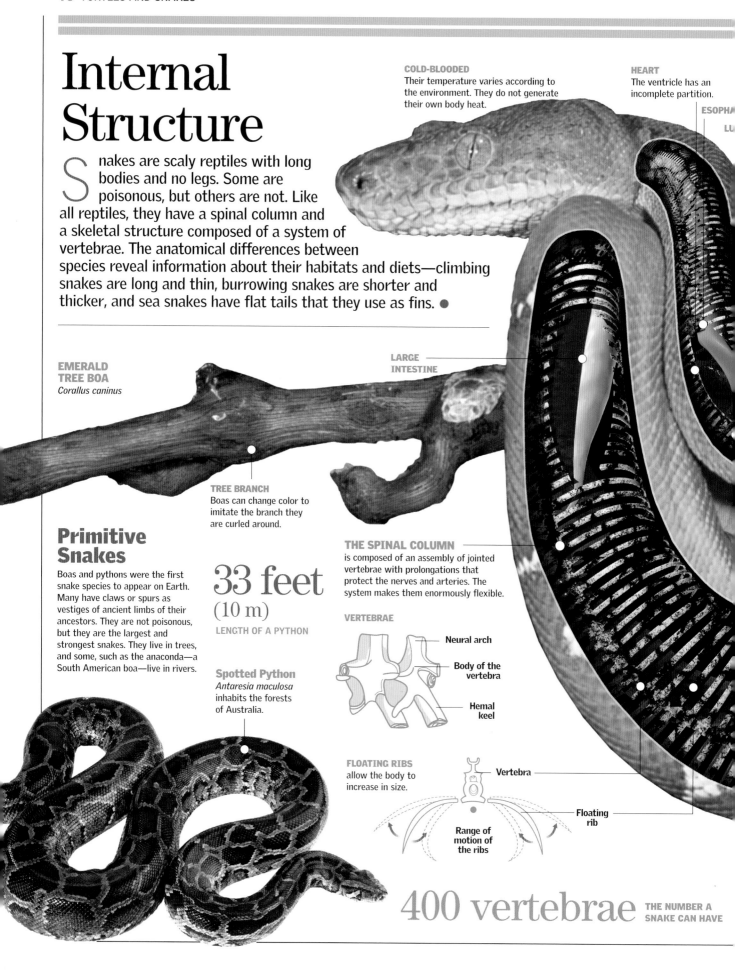

COLD-BLOODED
Their temperature varies according to the environment. They do not generate their own body heat.

HEART
The ventricle has an incomplete partition.

ESOPHA

LU

EMERALD TREE BOA
Corallus caninus

LARGE INTESTINE

TREE BRANCH
Boas can change color to imitate the branch they are curled around.

Primitive Snakes

Boas and pythons were the first snake species to appear on Earth. Many have claws or spurs as vestiges of ancient limbs of their ancestors. They are not poisonous, but they are the largest and strongest snakes. They live in trees, and some, such as the anaconda—a South American boa—live in rivers.

33 feet
(10 m)
LENGTH OF A PYTHON

Spotted Python
Antaresia maculosa inhabits the forests of Australia.

THE SPINAL COLUMN
is composed of an assembly of jointed vertebrae with prolongations that protect the nerves and arteries. The system makes them enormously flexible.

VERTEBRAE

Neural arch

Body of the vertebra

Hemal keel

FLOATING RIBS
allow the body to increase in size.

Vertebra

Floating rib

Range of motion of the ribs

400 vertebrae
THE NUMBER A SNAKE CAN HAVE

IVER
long and located
ong the esophagus.

BLADDER

STOMACH

SPLEEN

SCALES
are generally
found in the
dorsal region.

IDENTIFICATION OF SOME POISONOUS AND NONPOISONOUS VIPERS

TAIL
Suddenly
narrows (like a
rattle) but does
not end in a point

POISONOUS

HEAD Typically
wide and triangular

BODY
Relatively long
and rough

NONPOISONOUS

HEAD Typically narrow; hard
to distinguish from the neck

BODY
Narrow, with
smooth scales

TAIL
Narrows
gradually and
ends in a point

"Blind" Snakes

Some subtropical and tropical
snake species live underground
and only come out in droughts or
floods. These are the smallest
snakes; some are no longer than 4
inches (10 cm). They have large
heads, few teeth, and bodies
covered in very soft, slippery
scales, which enable them to slide
into anthills and termite hills,
their only sources of food. Their
eyes, which are covered with
scales, barely work.

**SMALL
INTESTINE**
is divided into a
small tract and a
large tract, which
ends well before
the tip of the tail.

SKIN
Many species of
snake have no scales
on the underside.

OVARIES
The female
reproductive
organs

TYPES OF MOVEMENT DEPENDING ON HABITAT

RECTILINEAR
Rainbow Boa

SIDEWINDING
Desert Snakes

SERPENTINE
King Cobra

CONCERTINA
Rattlesnake

Sophisticated Snakes

Snakes of the family Viperidae, as well as other
poisonous snakes that appeared later, have highly
acute senses and a mouth apparatus
with a system of retractable
fangs for injecting
venom.

INFRARED PITS
Snakes of the family Viperidae
are distinguished by two
thermoreceptive pits on either
side of their heads, which
enable them to sense
differences in temperature.
Some pits are extremely
sensitive, helping the snake
to gauge the size of its
prey when it hunts
at night.

REPRODUCTION
is sexual, and most
species lay eggs. Some
species give birth to
live young.

2,978

SNAKE SPECIES EXIST.

GABOON VIPER
Bitis gabonica

Deadly Embrace

Snakes have developed a wide range of techniques to kill their prey. For example, both boas and pythons are powerful constrictors, meaning that they kill by asphyxiating their prey rather than poisoning them with venom. Although boas and pythons belong to the same category of snakes (a category that includes the largest species in the world—the famous anaconda and reticulated python of Africa and Asia), their reproductive systems differ from one another. Their large size makes them heavy and slow moving, so they are easy prey for hunters, who kill them for their hides and meat.

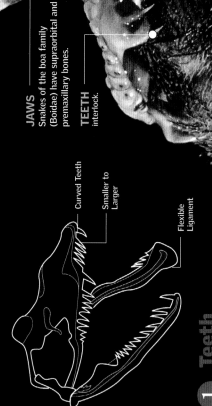

SCALES
Heat-sensitive

JAWS
Snakes of the boa family (Boidae) have supraorbital and premaxillary bones.

TEETH
interlock.

Curved Teeth

Smaller to Larger

Flexible Ligament

1 Teeth

The snake seeks out the head of its victim so that its prey will not be able to fight back. It takes the prey with its curving front teeth, keeping its victim from escaping. This enables it to suffocate its prey by coiling itself around the prey's body and squeezing (constricting).

AMAZON TREE BOA

Corallus hortulanus

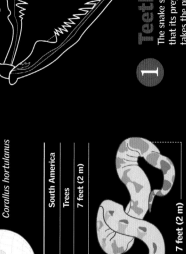

Range	South America
Habitat	Trees
Length	7 feet (2 m)

7 feet (2 m)

Tree Boa

can measure up to 7 feet (2 m) long and lives in trees. Its color blends in with the surrounding foliage, concealing it from predatory birds. Its prehensile tail holds firmly onto branches, while its head hangs down so that it can pounce on passing birds or mammals.

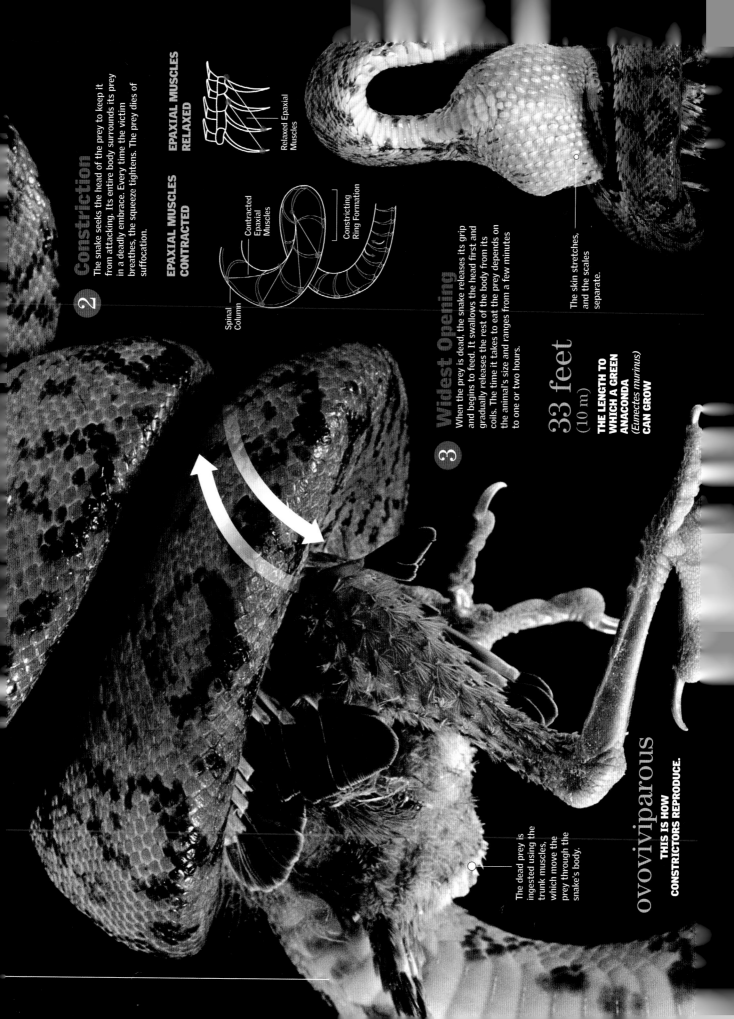

2 Constriction

The snake seeks the head of the prey to keep it from attacking. Its entire body surrounds its prey in a deadly embrace. Every time the victim breathes, the squeeze tightens. The prey dies of suffocation.

EPAXIAL MUSCLES CONTRACTED

EPAXIAL MUSCLES RELAXED

Relaxed Epaxial Muscles

Contracted Epaxial Muscles

Constricting Ring Formation

Spinal Column

3 Widest Opening

When the prey is dead, the snake releases its grip and begins to feed. It swallows the head first and gradually releases the rest of the body from its coils. The time it takes to eat the prey depends on the animal's size and ranges from a few minutes to one or two hours.

The skin stretches, and the scales separate.

33 feet (10 m)

THE LENGTH TO WHICH A GREEN ANACONDA (*Eunectes murinus*) **CAN GROW**

The dead prey is ingested using the trunk muscles, which move the prey through the snake's body.

ovoviviparous
THIS IS HOW CONSTRICTORS REPRODUCE.

A Specialized Mouth

The most primitive snakes have heavy skulls and few teeth. Most snakes, however, have lighter skulls and jointed jawbones. These joints are loose and can easily become dislocated so that the snake can swallow prey larger than the natural shape of its own head. The teeth are fixed in the upper jaw or the palate, and the fangs for injecting venom may be located either at the front or at the back of the mouth. Some species, as well as being large and powerful, have retractable fangs, allowing them to close their mouths when their fangs are not in use. ●

Cranial Anatomy

is directly related to each species' diet and—in the case of venomous snakes—to its system for injecting poison. Most snakes have small skulls with jawbones that can be separated voluntarily by sliding them along a kind of perpendicular rail, which consists of a bone called the quadrate. This greatly increases the size of the snake's mouth.

JACOBSON'S ORGAN gives the snake an excellent sense of smell. It consists of two cavities in the palate, into which the snake brings its tongue after "tasting" the outside air. That is why snakes continually stick out their tongues.

DUVERNOY'S GLAND

RETRACTOR MUSCLE

FANGS

GLOTTIS

UPPER JAW

1 Viperid

This type of skull has small teeth and large, retractable fangs that are thick or hooked.

QUADRATE

FUSED BONES

TEETH

The Deadliest Weapon

Rattlesnakes have long, thick fangs that are very sharp and kept folded inside their mouths. A movable joint at the base of the fang enables it to stand upright when the snake's mouth opens to bite.

LENGTHWISE
The venom flows through the tube and directly into the prey.

Entrance

Exit

CROSS SECTION
The tooth has a cavity that serves as the canal for the poison.

Poison Canal

Primitive Snakes

Boas and pythons are called primitive, since they have neither fangs nor venom. These snakes have several rows of small, inward-curving teeth used for holding prey and swallowing quickly without letting the prey worm out. This feature is necessary for the snakes to be able to hold onto their prey, since they lack venom. Venomous snakes, on the other hand, have little need to worry about their prey escaping, since they know that, after it is injected with the toxic substance, it will not be able to get very far.

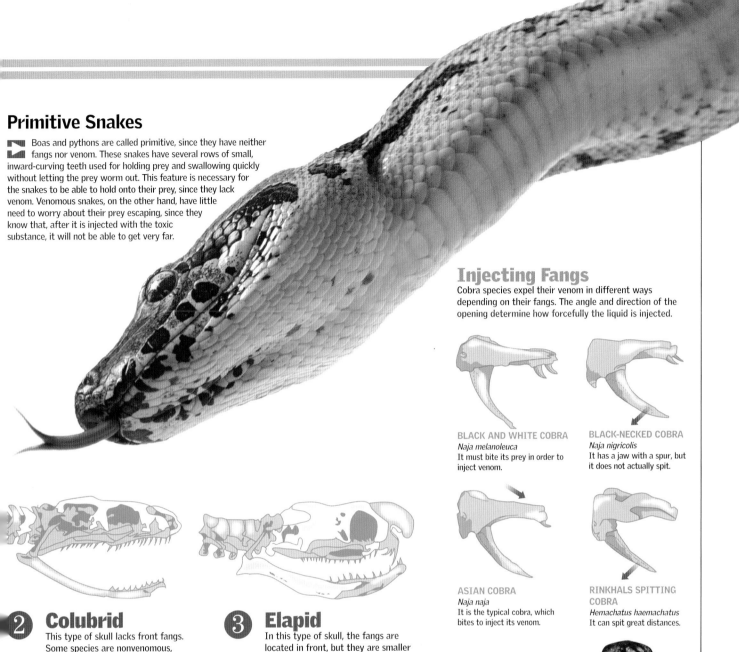

Injecting Fangs

Cobra species expel their venom in different ways depending on their fangs. The angle and direction of the opening determine how forcefully the liquid is injected.

BLACK AND WHITE COBRA
Naja melanoleuca
It must bite its prey in order to inject venom.

BLACK-NECKED COBRA
Naja nigricolis
It has a jaw with a spur, but it does not actually spit.

ASIAN COBRA
Naja naja
It is the typical cobra, which bites to inject its venom.

RINKHALS SPITTING COBRA
Hemachatus haemachatus
It can spit great distances.

② Colubrid
This type of skull lacks front fangs. Some species are nonvenomous, but others have fangs with a groove for delivering venom.

③ Elapid
In this type of skull, the fangs are located in front, but they are smaller and have only a groove, rather than a canal, for injecting venom.

Venom System
onsists of the two Duvernoy's glands, one on ach side of the skull, which produce venom and re connected to the fangs. When biting, muscle ontractions exert pressure on the gland and ctivate the injection mechanism.

6.6 feet (2 m)
THE DISTANCE FROM WHICH THE SPITTING COBRA CAN KILL BY SPRAYING ITS VENOM

Spitting Venom
Forty cobra species can spray their venom from a distance. They spray in self-defense when they feel threatened. They can direct the stream into an enemy's eyes, causing grave damage or even death. The shape of their fangs is essential to this defense.

NON-SPITTING
The long canal points downward and has a beveled edge at the end. The stream loses momentum.

SPITTING
The canal's opening points forward and is narrow so that it can eject the venom more forcefully.

A SOLENOGLYPHS
The hollow fangs are the only teeth in the jaw. They are long and retractable and inject venom into the prey's tissues.

B PROTEROGLYPHS
Small fangs in the front of the jaw, fixed in position and with a rear groove for conducting venom

C OPISTHOGLYPHS
Fangs in the back, with no canal or groove. The prey must be held in place.

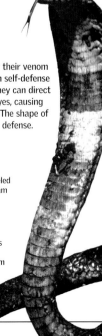

Cobras

Are an important group of snakes in the family Elapidae. Easily recognized by their outspread hoods, they are well known worldwide, mostly because of their use by snake charmers. Many cobra species carry deadly venom. Some can even spit from several yards away. Cobras of the *Naja* genus are the most widely recognized. They are widespread in Asia and were only recently recognized as 11 separate species. All are predatory; many eat only snakes. ●

SMOOTH
Cobra species have smooth scales.

Red Spitting Cobra
Naja pallida
One of 40 species of spitting cobras, it inhabits the Horn of Africa, where it is widely feared. It is distinguished by a black band below its neck.

BLACK BAND
It sets this species apart.

DISTRIBUTION OF *NAJA* SPECIES IN ASIA

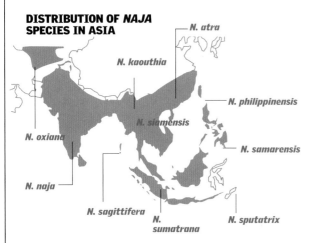

- *N. atra*
- *N. kaouthia*
- *N. philippinensis*
- *N. siamensis*
- *N. oxiana*
- *N. samarensis*
- *N. naja*
- *N. sagittifera*
- *N. sumatrana*
- *N. sputatrix*

HOW TO DISTINGUISH AMONG THEM

Although the Asian species look similar to one another, they often have distinguishing colors and scale patterns. The simplest way to identify them is by the pattern on their hoods—if you have time to look!

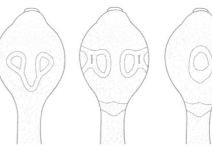

Indian Cobra
Naja naja

Chinese Cobra
Naja atra

Andaman Cobra
Naja sagittifera

Golden Spitting Cobra
Naja sumatrana

270

SPECIES OF ELAPIDS EXIST WORLDWIDE.

VENOM
is quite powerful. It paralyzes the muscles in minutes; the victim cannot flee and dies of cardiac arrest or asphyxiation.

ASIAN COBRA
Naja naja
It is the most widespread species on the Indian subcontinent and one of the best known. Its distinctive trait is the mark on its hood, similar to a pair of glasses, which gives this snake its other name: spectacled cobra.

BANDS
are usually found on the belly.

The Hood

It is believed that when cobras feel threatened or are about to attack, they spread their hoods by widening their necks in order to look larger than they actually are. The mechanism involves the ribs, which are widened by the muscles that lie between them. When cobras put on this display, they are ready to strike. Some species also hiss while in this position.

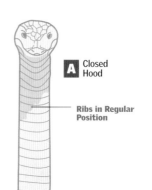

A Closed Hood

Ribs in Regular Position

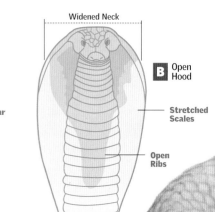

Widened Neck

B Open Hood

Stretched Scales

Open Ribs

MONOCLED COBRA
Naja kaouthia
This Asian species has soft scales. Its color varies widely depending on the region. One of its distinctive traits is the "monocle" on its hood, which gives it its common name.

MONOCLE
Made of two concentric rings, it is easily recognizable because of its white color.

SCALES
are soft to the touch.

BAND
is also distinctive in this species.

BACK
The scales are closer together.

11.5-16 feet (3.5-5 m)

3 feet (1 m): height when erect

KING COBRA
Ophiophagus hannah
This is the largest cobra, measuring between 11.5 and 16 feet (3.5-5 m). It can attack backward and raise its head more than 3 feet (1 m) above the ground.

Parietal Scales

Dorsal Scales

TOP VIEW

Sublabial Scales

Ventral Scales

BOTTOM VIEW

Arrangement of Scales

The appearance of the scales is a simple and easy way to classify species. The large parietal scales follow a line that usually differs among species. The sublabial scales are also widely used in identification. Usually there are five, but the number varies between species. The ventral scales are perhaps most easily used for identification, because they differ notably from one group to another. They are always wide, cover the entire body, and are divided into sections: neck, belly, and tail.

Ocular Scales

Lateral Scales

PROFILE

Egg Eaters

The egg-eating snake is both harmless and common. Its body is about as thick as an adult's fourth finger. The egg-eating snake eats bird eggs and hen eggs that are larger than its body. Although it might be confused with a true viper because of its size and coloring, it is classified as an oophagous (egg-eating) snake in the family *Dasypeltis*. Snakes in this family are distinguished by special vertebrae that help break the shell of an egg as it is swallowed. It selects eggs very carefully, using its highly refined sense of smell to make sure that they are not rotten. ●

Unique Diet

These snakes do not find eggs every day, so they regurgitate the shells to create more space in their stomachs for the eggs they will find in the future.

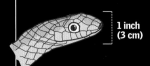

1 inch
(3 cm)

2 inches
(6 cm)

The folds in the snake's mouth hold the egg, moving it toward the throat.

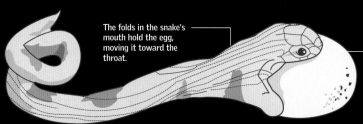

The egg slowly enters the mouth until it is completely inside.

SIZE COMPARISON
The egg is two to four times wider than the snake's body.

The interlocking scales separate when the skin is stretched.

1 Ingestion
The snake starts to swallow the egg in successive motions. The jaw opens wider and wider, and the skin on the throat becomes distended.

The egg is tough and does not break until it reaches the bony spines.

The throat returns to its normal position.

15 minutes
THE TIME IT TAKES TO SWALLOW AN EGG

2 Rupture
The egg reaches the esophageal teeth, which puncture the eggshell; the head and neck muscles then crush it.

A valve blocks the passage of eggshell fragments.

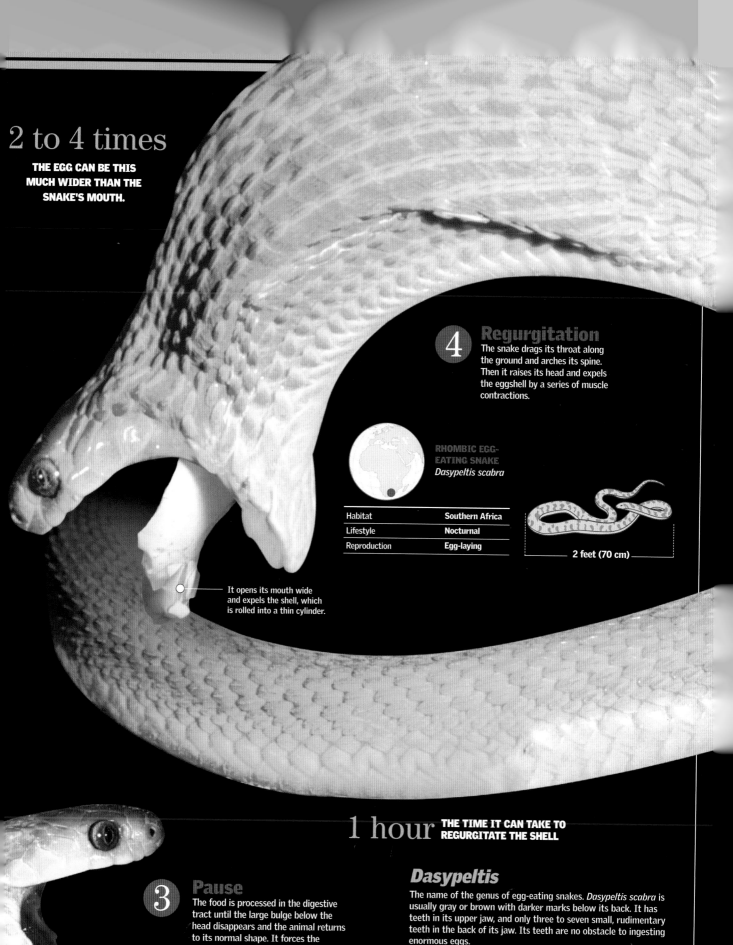

2 to 4 times

THE EGG CAN BE THIS MUCH WIDER THAN THE SNAKE'S MOUTH.

4 Regurgitation

The snake drags its throat along the ground and arches its spine. Then it raises its head and expels the eggshell by a series of muscle contractions.

RHOMBIC EGG-EATING SNAKE
Dasypeltis scabra

Habitat	Southern Africa
Lifestyle	Nocturnal
Reproduction	Egg-laying

2 feet (70 cm)

It opens its mouth wide and expels the shell, which is rolled into a thin cylinder.

1 hour **THE TIME IT CAN TAKE TO REGURGITATE THE SHELL**

3 Pause

The food is processed in the digestive tract until the large bulge below the head disappears and the animal returns to its normal shape. It forces the eggshell back into its mouth.

Dasypeltis

The name of the genus of egg-eating snakes. *Dasypeltis scabra* is usually gray or brown with darker marks below its back. It has teeth in its upper jaw, and only three to seven small, rudimentary teeth in the back of its jaw. Its teeth are no obstacle to ingesting enormous eggs.

Humans
and Reptiles

Often feared by humans, snakes have long been the object of stories and myths; however, few people know what snakes are actually like. Since snakes are deaf, when they emerge from a charmer's basket, they are actually following the movement of the flute. Many snake species face extinction from persecution resulting from their

MUSIC IN MARRAKESH
The snake charmers that live in the plaza of this city are famous and evoke scenes from the book *The Thousand and One Nights*.

...angerous reputation, their valued skins, and the desire of some to keep them as pets. Most snakes are beneficial to humans because they limit the spread of harmful animals like rats. ●

Heroes and Villains

Since time immemorial, reptiles have been the subjects of myths and legends. They have also earned their own space in religious texts, where they are depicted as gods or lesser beings. They may symbolize the incarnation of evil in some cases or divinity in others. The snake and the crocodile, among others, have taken on lives of their own; they play an active role in the stories of many peoples and have been assigned unique, culturally specific meanings. ◉

RAINBOW SNAKE
Snakes hold a special meaning for the Australian Aborigines and have been depicted in myth both as the wind god and as the protector of people.

SNAKES
are what Medusa had on her head instead of hair.

MEDUSA
Legend says that those who looked into the eyes of Medusa would be turned to stone for eternity.

Religious Meaning
The toad, as a symbol in Christianity, appears to be directly related to deadly sins such as greed, lust, and gluttony. In Egypt, crocodiles were venerated, and valuable jewels were given in their honor. The snake is also mentioned in sacred Hebrew texts.

FIERCE
Aztec serpent from the 15th century, housed in the British Museum

EVE
The snake is associated with trickery and treason in the Old Testament. It is the snake that incited Eve to enter into sin in the Garden of Eden by convincing her to eat forbidden fruit.

QUETZALCÓATL
is the Nahuatl name for the Feathered Serpent. In the Aztec pantheon, Quetzalcóatl was the god of day, the creator of maize, the god of religious ceremonies, and the defender of priests.

SEBEK
was a god worshipped by the ancient Egyptians. He had the body of a human being and the head of a crocodile, and he was considered to be the creator of the Nile. It is said that he emerged from the waters of chaos during the creation of the world.

Range
Because they can be found virtually everywhere, reptiles have managed to infiltrate myths all over the world. They were venerated by the Inca and Aztec cultures in the Americas and were the object of legends in every corner of Asia. In China and Japan, the dragon with a snake's body represented earthly power, knowledge, and strength and was the bestower of health and good luck.

Representations

The engraving of a snake biting its tail to form a circle was the emblem of the so-called seal of Solomon that was used by theosophical societies. In Buddhism, the snake represents natural tendencies toward aggression. However, in medicine, it has long been associated with an ancient Greek symbol, the "rod of Asclepius," which had a snake coiled around it. Asclepius was the Greco-Roman god of healing.

SIVA
Known in India as the god of destruction, Siva is depicted holding a snake around his neck.

DRAGON
In classical mythology, the dragon is associated with the ideas of guardianship and protection.

SNAKE
The dragon with the body of a snake is invoked in China and Japan to drive away bad spirits.

DRAGON
Image found in the Thian Hock Keng Temple in Singapore. In Eastern cultures, the dragon is a mythical animal and can symbolize good as well as evil.

Sin
IS TIED TO A SNAKE IN CHRISTIAN THEOLOGY.

CROCODILE
There is evidence that, in the 5th century BC, the Egyptians raised crocodiles as pets. A crocodile lived in a tank in the temple of Sebek and was pampered with the finest of foods.

MUMMIFIED
When this crocodile died, it was embalmed and placed in a sarcophagus surrounded by its own hoard of treasures.

Enchanted Snakes

Cobras, as well as vipers and boas (to a lesser degree), are the object of the fascinating performances of snake charmers. In Asia—especially India—snake charmers carry out a very dramatic performance that has been repeated since ancient times. Snake charming has since spread all the way to the Mediterranean coast of Africa. The technique of enchanting snakes requires a knowledge of their weaknesses. For example, it is the movement of the flute, not its actual sound, to which they respond.

A Historical Practice

Revered since antiquity, the charming of snakes is a tradition that had its golden age during the period of imperial expansion, when the West colonized the East. Snake charmers were considered exotic, and they traveled the world and performed at fairs in large cities. They became veritable ambassadors of the East.

LOW ACTIVITY
The basket is kept in the shadows. This causes the snakes to be less active, because they are not being warmed by the sun.

Snake charmers assume a crouching position for the performance.

The flute is called a *been* or a *pungi.*

The snakes appear.

The cobras dance.

1/3 of the snake's body

1 CALL

The flute is brought closer to the basket to call the cobra. Location is key. A cobra cannot reach beyond the portion of its body that is elevated.

India Sanctions Snake Charming

In 2004, snake charmers in India were able to resume their jobs after having been accused of mistreating their animals during their shows.

2 EXIT

The movement of the flute incites the cobra to extend its body.

3 DANCE

At the moment of greatest bodily extension, the cobra performs a dance that climaxes with the snake charmer kissing it on the top of its head.

A FAMILY TRADITION
The practice of snake charming is passed from fathers to sons. In Bangladesh, charmers even form their own community; most are of Bedey ethnicity.

FLUTE
Its movement, not its sound, enchants the snake. Cobras, like all snakes, are deaf.

SNAKES
Cobras are usually used, but vipers and even boas can serve as alternatives.

Cobras

Unlike vipers, cobras are not capable of striking from a coiled position. This keeps them from attacking beyond the reach of the extended portion of their bodies.

Coiled Cobra

1/3 of its Body

Endangered

arine turtles are in danger of extinction. Their need to leave the water to breathe makes them very easy to catch. Females and their offspring are at the greatest risk because they build exposed nests on the shore where they can easily be attacked by hunters and egg collectors. Others die when they are trapped in fishing nets. Marine turtles' nesting sites are also at risk because of the effects of coastal urbanization. Artificial light drives females from the routes they naturally take to lay their eggs. The offspring suffer from the same problem and become confused, unable to find their way. ●

**LOGGERHEAD
SEA TURTLE**
*Caretta
caretta*

Status	Endangered
Habitat	Tropical Waters
Size	4 feet (120 cm)

The loggerhead is a marine turtle that inhabits the coasts of tropical seas and can migrate great distances during its reproductive period. It lives in deep waters but is sometimes found near the shore. It is carnivorous but obtains food from a variety of sources depending on its age.

Migration

Some turtles travel great distances to reach the beaches where they will lay their eggs. The Laud turtle is capable of crossing the entire Atlantic Ocean.

HAWKSBILL TURTLE
Eretmochelys imbricata

Status	Critical
Habitat	Warm Atlantic
Size	2 to 2.5 feet (60-80 cm)

The hawksbill is one of the smallest sea turtles and is easily recognized by its shell, which has a central keel and toothed edges. The beautiful designs on their shells have caused this species to be savagely hunted. Hawksbills have a long life span and migrate less than other marine species.

LEATHERBACK SEA TURTLE
Dermochelys coriacea

Status	Endangered
Habitat	Tropical Waters
Size	4 to 6 feet (1.3-1.8 m)

The leatherback, the largest marine turtle, is one of the world's foremost migratory animals: it routinely crosses the Atlantic Ocean. The beaches where they nest and lay their eggs are now threatened by development related to tourism.

MESOAMERICAN RIVER TURTLE
Dermatemys mawii

Status	Endangered
Habitat	Central America and Mexico
Size	1.5 to 2 feet (50-65 cm)

Although turtles have developed adaptations for swimming, such as palm-shaped feet and a hydrodynamic shell, they are practically defenseless on land. They have very short tails, and the females have olive green coloring on the upper portions of their heads. They lay between six and 20 eggs in the marshy banks of rivers and are hunted by coypu (nutria) and humans.

GREEN SEA TURTLE
Chelonia mydas

Status	Endangered
Habitat	Tropical Waters
Size	3 feet (1 m)

The green sea turtle is one of the most common sea turtles. It is found in tropical and subtropical waters around the world. It has been a primary victim of commercial fishing. Green sea turtles are also in peril because of changing conditions on the beaches where they mate.

PACIFIC RIDLEY
Lepidochelys olivacea

Status	Endangered
Habitat	Gulf of Mexico
Size	1.5 to 2.5 feet (50-75 cm)

The Pacific ridley (olive ridley) has a round-shaped greenish-gray shell with five costal scutes. Its mouth is beaklike, similar to that of a parrot, and its preferred diet consists of crustaceans and benthic mollusks. It is the smallest of the sea turtles and the species under the greatest threat of extinction.

PANCAKE TORTOISE
Malacochersus tornieri

Status	Vulnerable
Habitat	East Africa
Size	5.5 to 7 inches (14-17 cm)

The shell of the pancake tortoise is not only very flat but also very flexible because of the openings in the bone on its underside. This feature allows it to crawl into narrow cracks to escape from predatory birds and mammals. It can also squeeze itself into holes.

GALAPAGOS TORTOISE
Geochelone nigra

Status	Vulnerable
Habitat	Galapagos Islands
Size	Up to 4 feet (1.2 m)

The shell and other characteristics of these tortoises have evolved in distinctive manners according to the conditions of each island where the species is found—especially conditions of climate and nutrition. Many have developed overgrown extremities to reach their food. They can no longer be found on some islands.

YELLOW-MARGINED BOX TURTLE
Cuora flavomarginata

Status	Endangered
Habitat	China, Taiwan
Size	8 inches (20 cm)

The population of this turtle has decreased significantly in recent decades because of the expansion of agriculture. The population remaining in Taiwan has stabilized and now shows signs of recovery. Those in China, on the other hand, remain in great danger.

Danger: Baits and Traps

S ea turtles are in danger of extinction. During their migrations, they eat the bait set on hooks intended for tuna. As the turtles fight to free themselves from the hooks, they damage their internal organs and lose their buoyancy, which causes them to die from asphyxiation. Fishing nets are also mortal traps for sea turtles. Certain governmental and private organizations are seeking ways to reduce the danger for these turtles and their future offspring. ●

Turtle Excluder Devices (TED)

▶ Sea turtles, such as the Laud, lay eggs on the Atlantic coasts of French Guiana and Suriname. They can only make it there, however, if they overcome the obstacle of deep fishing nets in the sea. To help them overcome this threat without interrupting the fishing of shrimp, nets have been developed with devices that exclude turtles from capture.

A Capture
The turtle swims in the ocean and is caught in the deep-sea net along with the shrimp that the nets are intended to capture.

B Escape
The turtles escape by swimming to the surface, where they can breathe.

Exclusion Exit

Dragging Net

The shrimp remain trapped in the net.

Turtle-Blocking Device

TED EFFICIENCY

85%
of turtles can escape from fishing nets using Turtle Excluder Devices.

15%
escape only with difficulty or remain trapped.

PROTECTION FOR TURTLE EGGS

The presence of humans on beaches interferes with the development of turtle offspring. In order to preserve turtles, countries have joined forces with environmental nongovernmental organizations to carry out different tasks. In Suriname, people gather the eggs to protect them from illegal traffickers and corral the nests so that tourists do not destroy them. In the Caribbean basin of Costa Rica, Tortuguero National Park was established in the region home to the greatest amount of spawning green turtles.

Annual Capture in the Atlant

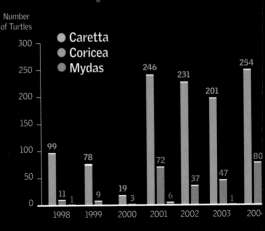

Number of Turtles

● Caretta
● Coricea
● Mydas

	1998	1999	2000	2001	2002	2003	200
	99	78	19	246	231	201	254
	11	9	3	72	37	47	80
	1			6		1	

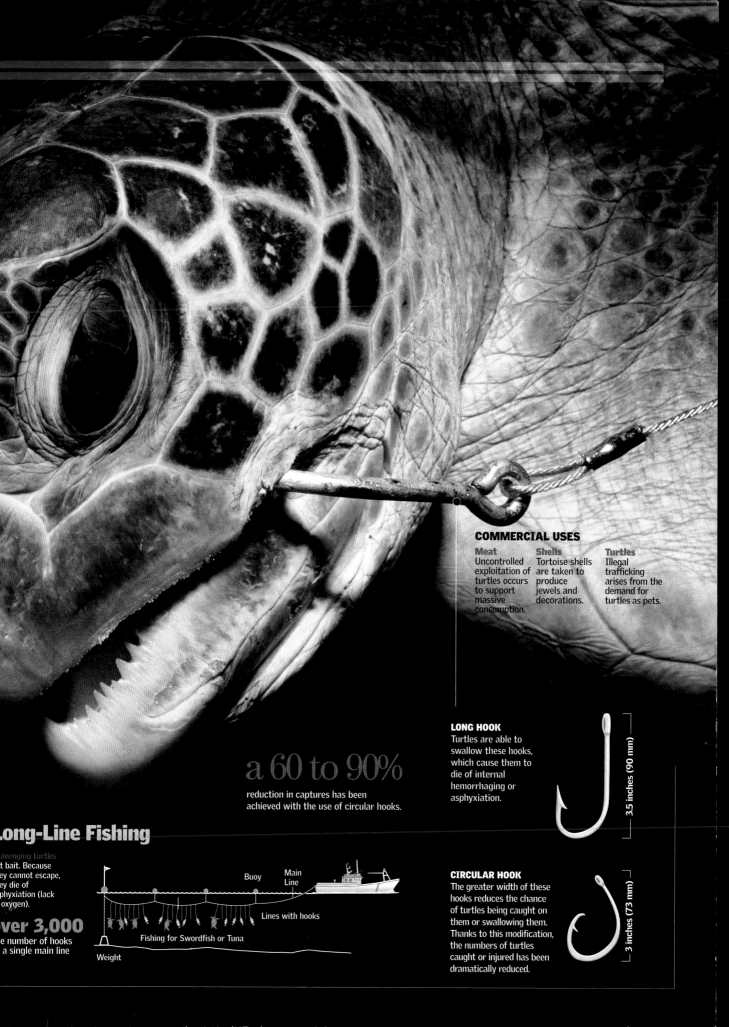

COMMERCIAL USES

Meat
Uncontrolled exploitation of turtles occurs to support massive consumption.

Shells
Tortoise shells are taken to produce jewels and decorations.

Turtles
Illegal trafficking arises from the demand for turtles as pets.

LONG HOOK
Turtles are able to swallow these hooks, which cause them to die of internal hemorrhaging or asphyxiation.

3.5 inches (90 mm)

CIRCULAR HOOK
The greater width of these hooks reduces the chance of turtles being caught on them or swallowing them. Thanks to this modification, the numbers of turtles caught or injured has been dramatically reduced.

3 inches (73 mm)

a 60 to 90%

reduction in captures has been achieved with the use of circular hooks.

Long-Line Fishing

avenging turtles
t bait. Because
ey cannot escape,
phyxiation (lack
oxygen).

ver 3,000
e number of hooks
a single main line

Buoy

Main Line

Lines with hooks

Fishing for Swordfish or Tuna

Weight

Fewer Each Time

any species of reptiles are at serious risk of extinction—mostly because of habitat loss caused by human activities. The most threatened species with the fewest resources for recovery are those native to islands, which are unable to emigrate or adapt to rapidly changing conditions. Urban growth, deforestation, and water contamination are among the principal forces that have created this critical situation. Conscious of the problem, many countries have developed legislation to protect reptiles, but it is not always effective.

ARUBA ISLAND RATTLESNAKE
Crotalus unicolor

Status	Critical
Habitat	Aruba
Size	3 feet (95 cm)

This rare, little-known species of rattlesnake inhabits an area of Aruba of roughly 30 square miles (76 sq km). Its current status as a critically endangered species is mostly due to the loss of its ecosystem. Between 1993 and 2004, only 185 specimens were sighted in the wild. Arikok National Park is currently developing programs for the snake's conservation.

GOLDEN FER-DE-LANCE
Bothrops insularis

Status	Critical
Habitat	Brazil
Size	2.6 feet (80 cm)

This viper inhabits just one small island on the Brazilian coast, only 106 acres (43 ha) in size, called Queimada Grande. Deforestation is its main threat. Although the snake's population is stable, the loss of its natural habitat places it in critical danger of extinction.

ARUBA ISLAND RATTLESNAKE
Crotalus unicolor

FIJI CRESTED IGUANA
Brachylophus vitiensis

BULGARDAGH VIPER
Vipera bulgardaghica

Status	Critical
Habitat	Turkey
Size	2.6 feet (80 cm)

This venomous, rodent-eating snake lives mostly in Anatolia. There its main threats are illegal trafficking and other human activities. Although awarded protected status in the region's animal preserves since 1994, it remains at serious risk of extinction.

FIJI CRESTED IGUANA
Brachylophus vitiensis

Status	Critical
Habitat	Fiji
Size	2.5 feet (75 cm)

The status of this species was last reviewed in 2003. It is distinguished by its rapid color changes and by the spiny crests on its back. It inhabits coastal forests, and its greatest threat is the introduction of goats to Fiji's islands. Since 1981, the island of Yaduataba has served as a primary sanctuary dedicated to its conservation. Nevertheless, the species continues to decline.

Habitat Loss

**THE LOSS OF HABITAT CAUSED BY HUMAN ACTIVITIES
IS THE MAIN CAUSE OF REPTILE EXTINCTION.**

HIERRO GIANT LIZARD
Gallotia simonyi

Status	Critical
Habitat	Canary Islands
Maximum Size	2 feet (60 cm)

This lizard inhabits the rocky outcroppings of El Hierro, one of the Canary Islands. Over recent decades, it was estimated that only 200 specimens remained, although the exact number is unknown. Its main cause of extinction is habitat loss and lack of food rising from competition with goats. Today these lizards are protected, and their numbers are recovering in preserves.

JAMAICA RACER
Alsophis ater

Status	Critical
Habitat	Jamaica
Size	2.8 feet (85 cm)

This reptile-eating snake inhabits the mountains of Jamaica. It is not venomous, and it is known for its great speed. Since 1994, it has been considered at critical risk of extinction because of habitat loss. Very few wild specimens have been sighted. Some experts believe that it may already be extinct.

TURKS AND CAICOS ROCK IGUANA
Cyclura carinata

Status	Critical
Habitat	Bahamas
Size	14 inches (36 cm)

Since the 1970s, nearly 13 subpopulations of iguanas have disappeared. Only one important species of this family of iguana remains, living in an area of 5 square miles (13 sq km) on a privately owned island. Its main threats come from predators introduced by humans and from habitat loss caused by urbanization.

CAPE DWARF CHAMELEON
Bradypodion pumilum

Status	Critical
Habitat	South Africa
Maximum Size	8 inches (20 cm)

This tiny, active chameleon is native to South Africa. As recently as a decade ago, it was commonly seen in thickets, in gardens, on plantations, and among crops. However, this species is currently at risk because of urban expansion. It is now only found on natural preserves.

CHINESE ALLIGATOR
Alligator sinensis

Status	Critical
Habitat	China
Maximum Size	6 feet (2 m)

This alligator inhabits the deep waters of the Yangtze River in China. Although its population is healthy in captivity, it is almost extinct in the wild. Today the Chinese government is developing a reintroduction program. Nevertheless, its future is uncertain.

Glossary

Adaptation

Trait of an organism's structure, physiology, or behavior that enables it to live in its environment.

Alkaline

Substances that increase the number of hydroxide ions (OH⁻) in a solution; having a pH greater than 7; basic; opposite of acidic.

Amino Acid

Organic molecule containing nitrogen in the form of ammonia ($NH2^-$) and a carboxyl group ($COOH^-$) joined to the same carbon atom. They form the building blocks of protein molecules.

Amphibian

Group of animals that today includes frogs, toads, salamanders, and limbless caecilians.

Ancestor

Parent, grandparent, or more remote forebear that transmits certain genetic characteristics to its descendants.

Antidote

Substance that neutralizes the action of a specific poison.

Antipoisonous Serum

Specially prepared substance used to neutralize toxins from the bite of a specific snake in persons who show signs of poisoning.

Aorta

Main artery in blood circulation systems. It sends blood to other tissues of the body.

Biped

Animal that stands upright, walks, or runs using only the two hind limbs.

Carbon-14

Radioactive carbon isotope whose concentration can help determine the age of fossils.

Carboniferous

Geological period during the Paleozoic Era, which took place between 360 and 251 million years ago.

Carnivore

Animal that obtains its nutrients and energy by eating flesh.

Carrion Eater

Animal that eats the flesh of a dead animal.

Cellular Membrane

Flexible lipid envelope covering all living cells. It contains cytoplasm and regulates the interchange of water and gases with the environment.

Cerebellum

A section of the brain in vertebrates located above the brain stem and behind and below the cerebrum. It coordinates muscular activity and maintains balance.

Chelonia

Collective term for land and sea turtles.

Chordate

Animal that belongs to the phylum Chordata; any animal having a spinal cord, whether throughout its development or only in certain stages. Animals that are not chordates are called invertebrates.

Chromosome

Structure that carries the genes and, in eukaryotic cells, is composed of filaments of chromatin that contract during mitosis and meiosis.

Class

Taxonomic group above order and below phylum. For example, the class Reptilia, within the phylum Chordata, contains orders such as Squamata and suborders such as Sauria.

Cloaca

Exit chamber of the digestive tract of reptiles and birds. In some species, it also functions as the site of the reproductive and excretory systems.

Cold-blooded

Organism whose body temperature is mainly controlled by an external heat source because it has little capacity to generate its own heat through its metabolism.

Connective Tissue

Tissue that joins, supports, and protects the other three types of tissues: epithelial, muscular, and nervous. It contains a network composed of many fibers surrounding the cells.

Coprolite

Fossilized animal excrement.

Cytoplasm

Fluid within the cell membrane.

Dental Battery

Set of teeth joined together to form a cutting and grinding surface.

Dermis

Internal layer of skin, located under the epidermis.

Dewlap

Fold of skin hanging below the chin and extending to the chest in some lizards and other tetrapods. It can be unfolded in territorial battles to intimidate or to display certain moods.

DNA

Deoxyribonucleic acid. Double-helix shaped molecule that contains encoded genetic information.

Duvernoy's Glands

System possessed by some snakes for injecting venom. They are a pair of modified salivary glands, one on either side of the head.

Efferent

Nerve or blood vessel that flows from a central point toward peripheral tissues or organs.

Egg

Fertilized ovule that develops into a new individual. It usually also refers to the entire structure that covers and protects the fertilized ovule.

Embryo

The first stage of development of a multicellular animal or plant.

Estivation

State of extreme lethargy or inactivity caused by prolonged periods of drought or excessive heat.

Evolution

Changes in the gene pool of a population caused by processes such as mutation, natural selection, and genetic drift.

Family

Taxonomic category lower than order and higher than genus. The family Viperidae, for example, groups together the vipers.

Fertilization

The joining of a female sex cell with a male sex cell to form a diploid zygote.

Fossil

Remains of various types of ancient life-forms, both plants and animals, in a rocky substrate. They are found in the geological strata of the Earth's surface.

Fossilization

Process by which a deceased organism becomes a fossil over thousands of years.

Gastrolith

Stone found in the stomachs of certain herbivorous dinosaurs that helped them crush and digest food.

Gene

Unit of information in a chromosome; sequence of nucleotides in the DNA molecule that carries out a specific function.

Genetic Drift

Change in the frequency of alleles, the result of random processes.

Genus

Taxonomic category that includes species.

Gills

Respiratory organs of aquatic animals. Often an extension of fine tissues from the outer surface of the body or, in vertebrates, from part of the digestive tract.

Gland

Group of epithelial cells that produce secretions, organized inside a covering membrane to form an organ whose function is to synthesize and excrete molecules that the organ itself does not use.

Gonads

Glands that produce reproductive sex cells.

Gondwana

Ancient southern supercontinent that broke up 180 million years ago to form Africa, South America, Australia, Antarctica, and India.

Gregarious

Animal whose typical behavior, as a species, is conducive to living in groups.

Herbivore

Animal that feeds on grass or other plants.

Inflammation

Nonspecific defensive reaction of the body to the invasion of a foreign substance or organism, frequently accompanied by the accumulation of pus and an increase in the temperature of the affected area.

Jacobson's Organ

Organ on the upper part of the palate that takes in substances captured by a reptile's tongue and analyzes them to determine various characteristics of the object they come from. Also called the vomeronasal organ.

Lability

Fragility of an organ; sensitivity to potentially destructive agents.

Lamarck, Jean-Baptiste

French naturalist (1744-1829). He was the first to propose a theory to explain the changes in living beings.

Laurasia

Ancient northern supercontinent formed of North America, Europe, and Asia, excluding India.

Lipids

Group of water-insoluble substances, including fats, oils, waxes, steroids, glycolipids, phospholipids, and carotenes.

Mammals

Vertebrate animals whose females have mammary glands, which secrete substances that serve as food for their young.

Mass Extinction

Brief geological interval in which the extinction rate is greatly increased, affecting a large number of species and causing a considerable reduction of biodiversity.

Metabolism

The sum of all the physical and chemical transformations that occur within a cell or organism.

Mimicry

A superficial similarity in shape, color, or behavior on the part of certain organisms (mimetics) to others (models) or to objects in the environment for the purpose of hiding, seeking protection, or some other benefit.

Mitosis

Nuclear cell division, in which two daughter nuclei are formed that are identical to the parent nucleus.

Molars

Group of teeth that crush food within the mouth.

Molecular Clock

Marker used to estimate the evolutionary distance between two species. It is evaluated by comparing the gradual accumulation of amino acids between the proteins of those species.

Nucleic Acid

Molecule carrying the genetic information of a cell.

Omnivore

Animal that feeds on animal and plant species

Opisthoglyph

Group of snakes with fangs located in the back of the upper jaw and smaller teeth in front. The fangs can be smooth or have a groove on the surface that enables secretions to flow into the wound they produced.

Order

Taxonomic category below class and above suborder and family. For example, snakes and saurian reptiles belong to the order Squamata.

Ovary

Organ that produces eggs (female sex cells).

Oviparous

Animal that reproduces by laying eggs.

Ovoviviparous

Animal that reproduces by forming eggs that are carried, with soft shells, inside the female until they hatch. They may hatch inside the mother and come out as if they had been born live or be expelled from the egg pouch, breaking its membrane in order to hatch.

Ovum

A female haploid reproductive cell. It contains half as many chromosomes as the parent cell.

Parasite

Organism that lives at the expense of another and typically obtains nutrients that have already been processed by the host.

Parthenogenesis

Form of asexual reproduction in certain species, such as the gecko, in which the females produce young (all or mostly females) without the intervention of a male.

Pheromones

Chemical substances secreted by the reproductive glands of certain animals in order to attract individuals of the opposite sex.

Photoperiod

Relative length of night and day that enables organisms to measure the change of seasons and that influences their behavior and physiology.

Phylogeny

Evolutionary history of any taxonomic group. Usually represented as a branching tree.

Piscivore

Animal that eats only fish.

Plastron

Lower part of the shell of a turtle or tortoise.

Predator

Animal that captures and eats other animals as prey.

Protein

Macromolecule composed of one or more chains of amino acids. They define the physical characteristics of an organism and, when acting as enzymes, regulate chemical reactions.

Proteroglyph

System of fangs in cobras, mambas, coral snakes, and sea snakes; or the name referring to the group that contains these types of snakes. The fangs are located in the front of the upper jaw and are hollow or have a surface groove for carrying venom. They are relatively short and are fixed in an extended position.

Protractile

Describes a type of reptilian tongue that can be voluntarily hurled outward in an extremely rapid, precise movement.

Reabsorption

Process in which substances that are filtered or secreted by the kidneys and which are necessary for maintaining the organism's internal equilibrium are reincorporated into the plasma.

Reflex

Simple action of the nervous system that involves a sensory neuron, often one or more interneurons, and one or more motor neurons.

Sensory Receptors

Cells, tissues, or organs that detect internal or external stimuli.

Sexual Reproduction

Reproduction based on the fertilization of a female sex cell by a male sex cell, resulting in the production of descendants different from either parent.

Shedding

Sloughing off or change of skin, a process that happens naturally in many reptiles.

Smooth Muscle

Non-striated muscle that covers the walls of the hollow organs and arteries and is controlled involuntarily.

Solenoglyph

System of long, hollow fangs in some snakes or the name of the group that refers to snakes possessing this characteristic. The fangs are the only teeth in the upper jaw, and they pivot so that they lie flat along the roof of the mouth when the mouth is closed. They inject venom deep into the tissues of prey.

Species

Biological concept of a group of organisms that can or do interbreed in the wild and are reproductively isolated from other similar groups. This biological concept should be distinguished from the concept of a species as a category and as a taxon.

Sperm Cell

Mature male sex cell, which is typically mobile and smaller than the female sex cell.

Spinal Cord

Part of the central nervous system of vertebrates, surrounded by the spinal column.

Striated Muscle

Muscle tissue with a striped appearance that shows the arrangement of the contracting elements. Includes the voluntary skeletal muscle and the cardiac muscle.

Thalamus

Part of the prosencephalon of vertebrates located behind and below the cerebrum. It is the main connection center between the brain stem and the upper cerebral regions.

Thermoregulation

Ability of reptiles to change their body temperature by moving from a warm place to a cooler one or vice versa.

Tissue

Group of identical cells that carry out a common function.

Trophic Level

The position of a species in the food web or food chain.

Uric Acid

Water-insoluble nitrogenated waste product; the main component of the excrement of reptiles and insects.

Vertebrates

Animals with a spinal column that provides a structural axis and develops around the notochord, completely replacing it in most species.

Viviparous

Animal species whose females do not lay eggs and whose young are born live.

Warm-blooded

Organism whose main heat source is internal and is produced largely through oxidative metabolism.

Zoonosis

Illness transmitted by animals to humans.

Index